Problem Solving Workbook

with Reading Strategies

Harcourt Brace & Company

Orlando • Atlanta • Austin • Boston • San Francisco • Chicago • Dallas • New York • Toronto • London

http://www.hbschool.com

CONTENTS

Getting Ready for Grade 2

1	Sums to 10	PS4
2	Order Property	PS5
3	Zero Property	PS6
4	Counting On	PS7
5	Addition Practice	PS8
6	Differences Through 10	PS9
7	Subtracting All or Zero	PS10
8	Using Subtraction to Compare	PS11
9	Counting Back	PS12
10	Problem Solving • Make a Model	PS13

CHAPTER 1 — Addition Facts to 18

1.1	Doubles	PS14
1.2	More Doubles	PS15
1.3	Adding on a Ten-Frame	PS16
1.4	Make a Ten	PS17
1.5	Adding Three Addends	PS18

CHAPTER 2 — Subtraction Facts to 18

2.1	Relating Addition and Subtraction	PS19
2.2	Subtracting on a Number Line	PS20
2.3	Fact Families	PS21
2.4	Missing Addends	PS22
2.5	Reading Strategy • Visualize	PS23

CHAPTER 3 — Numbers to 100

3.1	Grouping Tens	PS24
3.2	Tens and Ones to 50	PS25
3.3	Tens and Ones to 100	PS26
3.4	Reading Strategy • Matching Pictures to Text	PS27
3.5	Exploring Estimation	PS28

CHAPTER 4 — Number Patterns

4.1	Skip-Counting by Fives and Tens	PS29
4.2	Skip-Counting by Twos and Threes	PS30
4.3	Even and Odd Numbers	PS31
4.4	Counting On and Back by Tens	PS32
4.5	Reading Strategy • Make Predictions	PS33

CHAPTER 5 — Using Numbers to 100

5.1	Comparing Numbers	PS34
5.2	Greater Than and Less Than	PS35
5.3	After, Before, Between	PS36
5.4	Ordinal Numbers	PS37
5.5	Reading Strategy • Use Graphic Aids	PS38

CHAPTER 6 — Counting Money

6.1	Pennies, Nickels, and Dimes	PS39
6.2	Nickels, Dimes, and Quarters	PS40
6.3	Counting Collections	PS41
6.4	Counting Half-Dollars	PS42
6.5	Reading Strategy • Use Pictures	PS43

CHAPTER 7 — Using Money

7.1	Combinations of Coins	PS44
7.2	Equal Amounts Using Fewest Coins	PS45
7.3	Comparing Amounts to Prices	PS46
7.4	Making Change	PS47
7.5	Reading Strategy • Use Word Clues	PS48

CHAPTER 8 — Time on the Clock

8.1	Hour and Half-Hour	PS49
8.2	Telling Time to 5 Minutes	PS50
8.3	Telling Time to 15 Minutes	PS51
8.4	Practice Telling Time	PS52
8.5	Reading Strategy • Use Word Clues	PS53

CHAPTER 9

Time: Days, Weeks, Months

9.1	Reading a Calendar	PS54
9.2	Using a Calendar	PS55
9.3	Early or Late	PS56
9.4	Sequencing Events	PS57
9.5	Reading Strategy • Use Graphic Aids	PS58

CHAPTER 10

Exploring Two-Digit Addition

10.1	Regrouping Ones as Tens	PS59
10.2	Modeling One-Digit and Two-Digit Addition	PS60
10.3	Modeling Two-Digit Addition	PS61
10.4	Recording Two-Digit Addition	PS62
10.5	Reading Strategy • Visualize	PS63

CHAPTER 11

More Two-Digit Addition

11.1	Adding One-Digit and Two-Digit Numbers	PS64
11.2	Adding Two-Digit Numbers	PS65
11.3	More About Two-Digit Addition	PS66
11.4	Addition Practice	PS67
11.5	Reading Strategy • Noting Details	PS68

CHAPTER 12

Exploring Two-Digit Subtraction

12.1	Regrouping Tens as Ones	PS69
12.2	Modeling One-Digit and Two-Digit Subtraction	PS70
12.3	Recording Subtraction	PS71
12.4	Recording Two-Digit Subtraction	PS72
12.5	Reading Strategy • Use Word Clues	PS73

CHAPTER 13

More Two-Digit Subtraction

13.1	Subtracting One-Digit from Two-Digit Numbers	PS74
13.2	Two-Digit Subtraction	PS75
13.3	Practicing Two-Digit Subtraction	PS76
13.4	Using Addition to Check Subtraction	PS77
13.5	Reading Strategy • Use Pictures	PS78

CHAPTER 14

Organizing Data

14.1	Tally Tables	PS79
14.2	Reading Strategy • Use Graphic Aids	PS80
14.3	Taking a Survey	PS81
14.4	Comparing Data in Tables	PS82

CHAPTER 15

Making and Reading Graphs

15.1	Picture Graphs	PS83
15.2	Pictographs	PS84
15.3	Horizontal Bar Graphs	PS85
15.4	Reading Strategy • Use Graphic Aids	PS86

CHAPTER 16

Data and Predictions

16.1	Certain or Impossible	PS87
16.2	Interpreting Outcomes of Games	PS88
16.3	Most Likely	PS89
16.4	Less Likely	PS90

CHAPTER 17

Solid and Plane Figures

17.1	Identifying Solids	PS91
17.2	Sorting Solid Figures	PS92
17.3	Reading Strategy • Make Predictions	PS93
17.4	Making Plane Figures	PS94

CHAPTER 18

Plane Figures

18.1	Plane Figures	PS95
18.2	Sides and Corners	PS96
18.3	Separating to Make New Figures	PS97
18.4	Congruent Figures	PS98

CHAPTER 19 Symmetry

19.1	Line of Symmetry	PS99
19.2	More Symmetry	PS100
19.3	Moving Figures	PS101
19.4	More About Moving Figures	PS102

CHAPTER 20 Length: Customary Units

20.1	Using Nonstandard Units	PS103
20.2	Measuring with Inch Units	PS104
20.3	Using an Inch Ruler	PS105
20.4	Foot	PS106
20.5	Reading Strategy • Make Predictions	PS107

CHAPTER 21 Length, Perimeter, and Area

21.1	Centimeters	PS108
21.2	Decimeters	PS109
21.3	Exploring Perimeter	PS110
21.4	Reading Strategy • Make Predictions	PS111

CHAPTER 22 Capacity, Weight, and Temperature

22.1	Using Cups, Pints, and Quarts	PS112
22.2	More and Less Than a Pound	PS113
22.3	Using a Thermometer	PS114
22.4	Choosing the Appropriate Tool	PS115

CHAPTER 23 Fractions

23.1	Halves and Fourths	PS116
23.2	Thirds and Sixths	PS117
23.3	More About Fractions	PS118
23.4	Parts of Groups	PS119
23.5	Reading Strategy • Use Word Clues	PS120

CHAPTER 24 Numbers to 1,000

24.1	Groups of Hundreds	PS121
24.2	Numbers to 500	PS122
24.3	Numbers to 1,000	PS123
24.4	Reading Strategy • Noting Details	PS124
24.5	Building $1.00	PS125

CHAPTER 25 Comparing and Ordering Large Numbers

25.1	Greater Than	PS126
25.2	Less Than	PS127
25.3	Greater Than and Less Than	PS128
25.4	Before, After, and Between	PS129
25.5	Ordering Sets of Numbers	PS130

CHAPTER 26 Adding and Subtracting Large Numbers

26.1	Modeling Addition of Three-Digit Numbers	PS131
26.2	Adding Three-Digit Numbers	PS132
26.3	Modeling Subtraction of Three-Digit Numbers	PS133
26.4	Subtracting Three-Digit Numbers	PS134
26.5	Reading Strategy • Use Word Clues	PS135

CHAPTER 27 Multiplication

27.1	Adding Equal Groups	PS136
27.2	Multiplying with 2 and 5	PS137
27.3	Multiplying with 3 and 4	PS138
27.4	Reading Strategy • Recognize Patterned Text	PS139

CHAPTER 28 Division

28.1	How Many In Each Group?	PS140
28.2	How Many Equal Groups?	PS141
28.3	Reading Strategy • Recognize Patterned Text	PS142
28.4	Reading Strategy • Visualize	PS143

Sums to 10

Draw a picture.
Write the sum.

1. There are 3 white cats.
   There are 2 gray cats.
   How many cats in all?

   $3 + 2 =$ __5__ cats

2. 5 dogs are playing.
   2 dogs are eating.
   How many dogs in all?

   $5 + 2 =$ _____ dogs

3. There is 1 mother bird.
   There are 6 baby birds.
   How many birds in all?

   $1 + 6 =$ _____ birds

Mark the correct answer.

4. Which addition sentence
   matches the picture?

   ○ $6 + 2 = 8$

   ○ $2 + 2 = 4$

   ○ $6 + 4 = 10$

   ○ $3 + 3 = 6$

5. Which addition sentence
   matches the picture?

   ○ $6 + 3 = 9$

   ○ $6 + 6 = 12$

   ○ $3 + 3 = 6$

   ○ $2 + 1 = 3$

Order Property

Write the sum.

1. Doug has 4 blue caps.
He has 5 red caps.
How many caps does
Doug have?

$4 + 5 =$ __*9*__ caps

2. Doug has 5 red caps.
He has 4 blue caps.
How many caps does
Doug have?

$5 + 4 =$ _____ caps

3. Carol has 3 blue buttons.
She has 2 green buttons.
How many buttons does
Carol have?

$3 + 2 =$ _____ buttons

4. Carol has 2 green buttons.
She has 3 blue buttons.
How many buttons does
Carol have?

$2 + 3 =$ _____ buttons

Mark the correct answer.

5. Which has the same sum as
$6 + 2$?

○ $4 + 5$
○ $8 + 2$
○ $2 + 6$
○ $4 + 2$

6. Which has the same sum as
$4 + 3$?

○ $3 + 4$
○ $3 + 3$
○ $4 + 4$
○ $7 + 3$

Zero Property

Write the sum.

1. Kay has 8 shells.
   Roy has no shells.
   How many shells do they
   have in all?

   ___8___ shells

2. Mason has no cars.
   His father has 1 car.
   How many cars do they
   have together?

   _____ car

3. Ted has 2 shirts.
   He buys 2 more.
   How many shirts does
   he have?

   _____ shirts

4. Tina has 3 dogs.
   Luke has 4 dogs.
   How many dogs do they
   have in all?

   _____ dogs

Mark the correct answer.

5. There are 3 apples on one
   tree. There are no apples
   on the other tree. How many
   apples are on both trees?

   ○ 0
   ○ 2
   ○ 3
   ○ 6

6. Mark caught 9 fish.
   Julie caught no fish.
   How many fish did they
   catch in all?

   ○ 0
   ○ 3
   ○ 6
   ○ 9

Counting On

Count on to find the sum.

1. There are 6 kites in the air.
   There are 2 kites on the ground.
   How many kites are there?

   $6 + 2 = \underline{8}$ kites

2. Joyce had 5 crayons.
   Larry gave her 1 crayon.
   How many crayons does Joyce have?

   $5 + 1 = \underline{\quad}$ crayons

3. Gary drew 4 pictures.
   Then he drew 2 more.
   How many pictures did Gary draw?

   $4 + 2 = \underline{\quad}$ pictures

4. There are 3 girls.
   There are 3 boys.
   How many children are there?

   $3 + 3 = \underline{\quad}$ children

Mark the correct answer.

5. Bella has 7 red pencils and 2 white pencils. How many pencils does Bella have?

   ○ 7

   ○ 9

   ○ 8

   ○ 10

6. There are 8 cats with tails and 2 cats with no tails. How many cats are there?

   ○ 2

   ○ 8

   ○ 6

   ○ 10

Addition Practice

Write the sum.

1. Amy bought

and .

$$3 + 4 = \underline{\quad 7 \quad} ¢$$

2. Grace bought

and  .

$$6 + 3 = \underline{\qquad} ¢$$

3. Jen bought

and  .

$$2 + 5 = \underline{\qquad} ¢$$

4. Gina bought

and .

$$4 + 2 = \underline{\qquad} ¢$$

Mark the correct answer.

5. Fred bought a truck for 8¢ and a car for 2¢. How much did Fred spend?

◯ 8¢   ◯ 9¢

◯ 10¢   ◯ 11¢

6. Will bought 2 balls for 4¢ each. How much did he spend?

◯ 8¢   ◯ 9¢

◯ 10¢   ◯ 11¢

Differences Through 10

Draw a picture.
Write the sum or difference.

1. Jane had 8 ducks.
   She gave away 5 ducks.
   How many ducks does
   she have?

   $8 - 5 = \underline{3}$ ducks

2. There are 6 ducks in the
   pond. I duck flies away.
   How many ducks are left?

   $6 - 1 = \underline{}$ ducks

3. There are 4 white ducks and
   4 black ducks. How many
   ducks are there?

   $4 + 4 = \underline{}$ ducks

Mark the correct answer.

4. There are 9 ducks in the
   water. I duck gets out.
   How many ducks are in
   the water?

   ○ 10
   ○ 9
   ○ 8
   ○ 7

5. There are 7 ducks playing.
   Then 2 ducks swim away.
   How many are still playing?

   ○ 4
   ○ 5
   ○ 9
   ○ 10

Subtracting All or Zero

Subtract.

1. There were 8 frogs by a pond. Then 5 frogs jumped away. How many frogs are left?

$$8 - 5 = \underline{} \text{ frogs}$$

2. There were 6 frogs on a log. Then all 6 frogs jumped off. How many frogs are left?

$$6 - 6 = \underline{} \text{ frogs}$$

3. There were 2 frogs on a rock. No frogs jumped off. How many frogs are on the rock?

$$2 - 0 = \underline{} \text{ frogs}$$

4. There are 5 frogs on a rock. 5 more frogs jump on. How many frogs are on the rock?

$$5 + 5 = \underline{} \text{ frogs}$$

Mark the correct answer.

5. There were 7 frogs. All 7 frogs hopped away. How many frogs are left?

○ 0

○ 1

○ 7

○ 14

6. Maria caught 3 frogs. None of the frogs got away. How many frogs does Maria have?

○ 0

○ 1

○ 3

○ 6

Using Subtraction to Compare

Use the pictures. Solve.

1. How many more gray fish than white fish are there?

$6 - 3 =$ __3__ more gray fish

---

2. How many more white birds than gray birds are there?

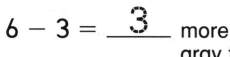

$5 - 2 =$ _____ more white birds

---

3. How many fish are there?

$3 + 6 =$ _____ fish

Mark the correct answer.

4. How many more ◯ than ▢ are there?

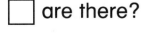

◯ 0   ◯ 2

◯ 1   ◯ 3

5. How many more ▢ than △ are there?

◯ 0   ◯ 2

◯ 1   ◯ 3

Counting Back

Solve.

1. Sue saw 8 birds. Then 2 birds flew away. How many birds are left?	$\underline{8}\ \ominus\ \underline{2}\ =\ \underline{6}$ birds	
2. Mom baked 3 apple pies. She baked 2 peach pies. How many pies did she bake?	___ ◯ ___ = ___ pies	
3. Brad had 9 grapes. He ate 2 grapes. How many grapes are left?	___ ◯ ___ = ___ grapes	
4. Ron washed 7 plates. He washed 5 cups. How many more plates than cups did he wash?	___ ◯ ___ = ___ more plates	

Mark the correct answer.

5. Leslie cleaned 6 shoes
and 4 boots. How many
more shoes than boots
did she clean?

  ◯ 2

  ◯ 4

  ◯ 10

  ◯ 14

6. There were 9 plates.
Rick put away 2 plates.
How many plates
are left?

  ◯ 5

  ◯ 7

  ◯ 11

  ◯ 12

Problem Solving • Make a Model

Use the four steps to solve the problem.

1. Cruz is 10 years old. His sister is 4 years old. How much older is Cruz than his sister?

$$\underline{10} \,\bigodot\, \underline{4} = \underline{6}$$
years older

2. Ruby is 2 years old. Joe is 6 years older than Ruby. How old is Joe?

$$\underline{\quad} \,\bigcirc\, \underline{\quad} = \underline{\quad}$$
years old

3. Don is 5 years old. How old will he be in 5 years?

$$\underline{\quad} \,\bigcirc\, \underline{\quad} = \underline{\quad}$$
years old

4. Tosha will be 10 years old in 3 years. How old is she now?

$$\underline{\quad} \,\bigcirc\, \underline{\quad} = \underline{\quad}$$
years old

Mark the correct answer.

5. Abe is 8 years old. Tammy is 7 years younger than Abe. How old is Tammy?

- ◯ 0
- ◯ 1
- ◯ 2
- ◯ 15

6. In 1 year Randy will be 9 years old. How old is he now?

- ◯ 7
- ◯ 8
- ◯ 10
- ◯ 19

Doubles

Draw a picture to show your answer.
Write the addition sentence.

1. Sam has 2 dogs. He has
   2 cats. How many animals
   does he have?

   __2__ + __2__ = __4__ animals

2. There are 6 muffins in 1 box.
   How many muffins are in
   2 boxes?

   _____ + _____ = _____ muffins

3. Jason had 9 fish. He bought
   9 more. How many fish does
   he have now?

   _____ + _____ = _____ fish

Mark the correct answer.

4. Which addition sentence
   matches the picture?

   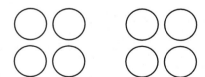

   ◯ 4 + 2 = 6

   ◯ 4 + 4 = 8

   ◯ 4 + 5 = 9

   ◯ 8 + 8 = 16

5. Which addition sentence
   matches the picture?

   ◯ 2 + 2 = 4

   ◯ 7 + 2 = 9

   ◯ 7 + 7 = 14

   ◯ 3 + 4 = 7

More Doubles

Draw a picture.
Solve.

I. Sue has 6 green apples and 7 red apples. How many apples does she have? ____13____ apples	
2. Ian has 3 dimes. Erika has I more dime than Ian. How many dimes do they have together? _____ dimes	
3. There are 5 people in a red car and 5 people in a green car. How many people in all? _____ people	
4. Amy collects 6 shells. Then she collects 6 more. How many shells does she collect? _____ shells	

Mark the correct answer.

5. Which is I more than 7 + 7?

- $\bigcirc$ 7 + 6
- $\bigcirc$ 7 + 8
- $\bigcirc$ 8 + 8
- $\bigcirc$ 6 + 6

6. Which is I less than 6 + 6?

- $\bigcirc$ 7 + 7
- $\bigcirc$ 6 + 7
- $\bigcirc$ 6 + 5
- $\bigcirc$ 5 + 5

Adding on a Ten-Frame

Use a ten-frame and counters.
Find the sum.

1. Dick drew 9 red birds.
   He drew 5 blue birds.
   How many birds did he draw?

   __9__ + __5__ = __14__ birds

2. Kim drew 7 cats and 8 dogs.
   How many animals did
   she draw?

   _____ + _____ = _____ animals

3. Toby drew 4 dogs. Gary drew
   9 more dogs than Toby. How
   many dogs did Gary draw?

   _____ + _____ = _____ dogs

4. Greg and Rose made 9 cards
   each. How many cards did
   they make together?

   _____ + _____ = _____ cards

Mark the correct answer.

5. There are 2 cats and 9
   dogs. How many animals
   are there?

   ○ 11   ○ 2

   ○ 7   ○ 9

6. Tom found 9 worms. Ed
   found 6 worms. How many
   worms did they find?

   ○ 3   ○ 12

   ○ 18   ○ 15

Name _____

Make a Ten

Draw a picture. Solve.

1. Mr. Long bought 8 red apples and 5 green apples. How many apples did he buy?

__13__ apples

2. Ted sees 6 red hens and 9 white hens. How many hens does he see?

_____ hens

3. Julie has 4 toy horses. She gets 4 more. How many horses does Julie have?

_____ horses

4. Ryan has 4 dogs and 7 cats. How many pets does Ryan have?

_____ pets

Mark the correct answer.

5. Jo has 3 dolls. Su has 6 more dolls than Jo. How many dolls does Su have?

○ 9
○ 6
○ 3
○ 8

6. Dave has $5. Bill has $9 more than Dave. How much money does Bill have?

○ $14
○ $15
○ $16
○ $10

Adding Three Addends

Solve. Use counters if needed.

1. Lin has 3 red fish, 4 blue fish, and 5 yellow fish. How many fish does Lin have?

   $\underline{3} + \underline{4} + \underline{5} = \underline{12}$ fish

2. Charlie has 3 blue boats, 2 red boats, and 3 yellow boats. How many boats does he have?

   ___ + ___ + ___ = _____ boats

3. Jason has 8 boats. He has 9 more rafts than boats. How many rafts does he have?

   ___ + ___ = _____ rafts

4. Kali has 5 big fish and 6 little fish. How many fish does she have?

   ___ + ___ = _____ fish

Mark the correct answer.

5. Ron has 1 red car, 4 green cars, and 5 blue cars. How many cars does he have?

   ○ 9   ○ 10

   ○ 11   ○ 12

6. Lisa sees 2 white birds, 4 black birds, and 3 brown birds. How many birds does she see?

   ○ 6   ○ 7

   ○ 8   ○ 9

Relating Addition and Subtraction

Add or subtract.
Draw a picture to show
your answer.

1. Judy has 12 cars.
   She gives 7 cars to Will.
   How many does she have left?

   $\underline{12}$ – $\underline{7}$ = $\underline{5}$ cars

2. Steve has 8 cars.
   Maria gives him 7 more.
   How many does he have now?

   _____ + _____ = _____ cars

3. Sam has 10 trucks.
   He loses 5 trucks.
   How many does he have left?

   _____ – _____ = _____ trucks

4. Vicki has 5 blue trucks
   and 9 red trucks. How
   many trucks does she have?

   _____ + _____ = _____ trucks

Mark the correct answer.

5. There are 13 ants on a log.
   Then 7 ants crawl away.
   How many ants are left?

   ○ 4   ○ 5

   ○ 6   ○ 7

6. There are 5 children.
   2 children are boys.
   How many are girls?

   ○ 1   ○ 3

   ○ 7   ○ 8

Subtracting on a Number Line

Subtract.
Use the number line.

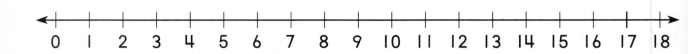

0 1 2 3 4 5 6 7 8 9 10 11 12 13 14 15 16 17 18

1. Patty has 8 apples.
She eats 2 apples.
How many are left?

_____6_____ apples

2. There are 16 carrots.
Juan eats 7 carrots.
How many are left?

_____ carrots

3. Lynn has 11 apples.
She eats 2 apples.
How many are left?

_____ apples

4. Greg has 18 grapes.
He eats 9 grapes.
How many are left?

_____ grapes

Mark the correct answer.

5. Jack has 8 flowers.
He gives 8 to his mom.
How many does Jack
have left?

◯ 0
◯ 1
◯ 8
◯ 16

6. There are 16 flowers.
8 flowers are yellow.
The other flowers are red.
How many flowers are red?

◯ 0
◯ 8
◯ 9
◯ 15

Fact Families

Write the fact family for the set of numbers.

1. Martha pulls 15 cubes out of a bag.
7 cubes are red and 8 cubes are blue.

$$\underline{7} + \underline{8} = \underline{15} \qquad \underline{8} + \underline{7} = \underline{15}$$

$$\underline{15} - \underline{7} = \underline{8} \qquad \underline{15} - \underline{8} = \underline{7}$$

2. Ann Lee pulls 11 cubes out of a bag.
5 cubes are yellow and 6 cubes are green.

$$\underline{} + \underline{} = \underline{} \qquad \underline{} + \underline{} = \underline{}$$

$$\underline{} - \underline{} = \underline{} \qquad \underline{} - \underline{} = \underline{}$$

3. Carol pulls 17 cubes out of a bag.
9 cubes are blue and 8 cubes are red.

$$\underline{} + \underline{} = \underline{} \qquad \underline{} + \underline{} = \underline{}$$

$$\underline{} - \underline{} = \underline{} \qquad \underline{} - \underline{} = \underline{}$$

Mark the correct answer.

4. Lin has 9 pennies. Leslie gives her 4 more. How many pennies does Lin have?

- ○ 5
- ○ 7
- ○ 13
- ○ 14

5. Which belongs in the fact family for the set of numbers?

4	5	9

- ○ $9 - 4 = 5$
- ○ $5 + 9 = 14$
- ○ $14 - 5 = 9$
- ○ $5 - 4 = 1$

Missing Addends

Draw a picture.
Complete the number sentence.

1. There are 17 horses on a farm.
   9 are inside the barn. How many
   are outside the barn?

   $9 + \underline{8} = 17$

   $\underline{8}$ are outside.

2. There are 5 white horses, 6
   brown horses, and 3 black horses.
   How many horses are there?

   $\underline{} + \underline{} + \underline{} = \underline{}$ horses

3. There are 7 mother horses.
   There are 7 baby horses.
   How many horses are there in all?

   $7 + \underline{} = \underline{}$ horses

Mark the correct answer.

4. Which number is the missing
   addend?

   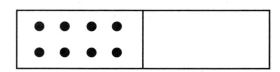

   $8 + \underline{} = 13$

   ○ 3 ○ 5

   ○ 8 ○ 13

5. Ed has 11 horses. 2 are
   black. The rest are brown.
   How many are brown?

   $2 + \underline{} = 11$

   ○ 7 ○ 9

   ○ 11 ○ 13

Reading Strategy • Visualize

Picturing a problem in your mind can help you solve
the problem.

Bob's Sport Shop has 9 red
balls and 7 blue balls for sale.
How many balls are for sale?

1. Read the problem.
   Picture the red balls
   and blue balls.

2. Draw a picture of the balls.

3. Write a number sentence.

   $9 + 7 =$ _____

4. Solve the problem.
   $9 + 7 = \underline{16}$ balls

Picture the problem.
Draw a picture to solve.

5. There are 15 players on the field.
   Then 9 players sit on the bench. How
   many players are still on the field?

   _____ players

6. There are 4 boys and 8 girls on the
   team. How many children are on
   the team?

   _____ children

Grouping Tens

Write how many tens.
Then write how many ones.

1.

__8__ tens = __80__ ones

2.

_____ tens = _____ ones

3.

_____ tens = _____ ones

4.

_____ tens = _____ ones

Mark the correct answer.

5. Vic ordered 30 pens. How many boxes of 10 pens did Vic order?

  ○ 3   ○ 10

  ○ 5   ○ 30

6. Cathy ordered 1 box of ten pens. How many pens did she order?

  ○ 1   ○ 50

  ○ 10   ○ 100

Tens and Ones to 50

Solve. Then draw a model.

1. Julie puts her rocks in 1 group of ten. She has 6 rocks left over. How many rocks does she have?

   __16__ rocks

2. There are 10 crayons in a box. Nick buys 2 boxes. How many crayons does he buy?

   _____ crayons

3. Josh puts his cars in 3 groups of ten. He has 3 cars left over. How many cars does he have?

   _____ cars

Mark the correct answer.

4. Which is the number?

   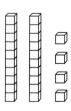

   ○ 20   ○ 24

   ○ 40   ○ 42

5. Which number has 4 tens and 9 ones?

   ○ 40   ○ 44

   ○ 49   ○ 94

Tens and Ones to 100

Write how many tens and ones.
Then write the number.

1.

_____6_____ tens _____3_____ ones = _____63_____ stamps

2.

_____ tens _____ ones = _____ stamps

3.

_____ tens _____ ones = _____ stamps

4.

_____ tens _____ ones = _____ stamps

Mark the correct answer.

5. Which is the number?

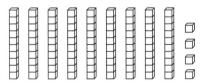

- ○ 49
- ○ 94
- ○ 13
- ○ 5

6. Which is the number?

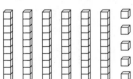

- ○ 55
- ○ 56
- ○ 65
- ○ 66

Reading Strategy • Matching Pictures to Text

Matching pictures to the words in a problem
can help you solve the problem.

Frank uses 10 blocks to build
each tower. How many blocks
does Frank have?

1. Read the problem.
   Look for important facts.

   There are 10 blocks in each tower.

2. Look at the picture. Match what you
   see in the picture with the words in
   the problem.

   There are 3 towers of 10 blocks.
   There are 4 blocks left over.

3. Solve the problem.

   The picture shows 3 tens and 4 ones.

   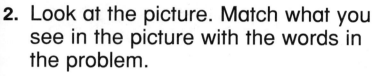
   Frank has __34__ blocks.

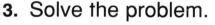

Match what you see in the picture
with the words in the problem.
Solve the problem.

4. Gina makes bracelets with
   10 beads each. How many
   beads does Gina have?

   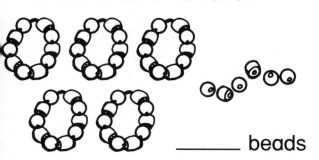

   _____ beads

5. Tony puts 10 crayons in
   each box. How many
   crayons does he have?

   _____ crayons

Exploring Estimation

Look at each group of beads.
Use these groups to help you choose the better estimate.

10 beads

25 beads

50 beads

1. About how many beads?

(about 25 beads)

about 50 beads

2. About how many beads?

about 25 beads

about 50 beads

3. About how many beads?

about 10 beads

about 25 beads

4. About how many beads?

about 10 beads

about 25 beads

Mark the correct answer.

5. About how many beads?

○ 10
○ 25
○ 50

6. About how many beads?

○ 10
○ 25
○ 50

Skip-Counting by Fives and Tens

Count by fives or tens.
Write the numbers.

1. Laura has 5 nickels. How much money does she have?

5¢,   10 ¢,   15 ¢,   20 ¢,   25 ¢

2. Cory has 8 dimes. How much money does he have?

10¢, ____¢, ____¢, ____¢, ____¢, ____¢, ____¢, ____¢

3. Mel has 8 nickels. How much money does he have?

5¢, ____¢, ____¢, ____¢, ____¢, ____¢, ____¢, ____¢

Mark the correct answer.

4. Count by tens. Which number comes next?

20, 30, 40, _____

○ 30   ○ 40

○ 50   ○ 60

5. Count by fives. Which is the missing number?

15, 20, _____, 30

○ 21   ○ 25

○ 29   ○ 35

Skip-Counting by Twos and Threes

Count by twos or threes.
Write the numbers.

1. Cammy has 5 cans of tennis balls. There are 3 balls in each can. How many tennis balls does she have?

3, __6__, __9__, __12__, __15__ tennis balls

2. Marilyn counts 8 bags of apples. There are 3 apples in each bag. How many apples does she count?

3, _____, _____, _____, _____, _____, _____, _____ apples

3. Darrell has 8 packs of socks. There are 2 socks in each pack. How many socks does he have?

2, _____, _____, _____, _____, _____, _____, _____ socks

Mark the correct answer.

4. Count by twos. Which numbers come next?

6, 8, 10, _____, _____

○ 11, 12   ○ 12, 14

○ 12, 15   ○ 9, 8

5. Count by threes. Which numbers come next?

3, 6, 9, _____, _____

○ 10, 11   ○ 11, 13

○ 12, 13   ○ 12, 15

Even and Odd Numbers

Draw the number of buttons.
Write **even** or **odd**.

1. Linda has 11 buttons. Does she have an even or odd number of buttons? _____odd_____	
2. Ian has 15 buttons. Does he have an even or odd number of buttons? _____	
3. Chris has 12 buttons. Does he have an even or odd number of buttons? _____	
4. Erika has 16 buttons. Does she have an even or odd number of buttons? _____	

Mark the correct answer.

5. Greg has 10 socks. Does he have an even or odd number of socks?

◯ even   ◯ odd

6. Leslie has 13 socks. Does she have an even or odd number of socks?

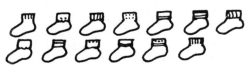

◯ even   ◯ odd

Counting On and Back by Tens

Count on or back by tens.
Solve.

1. David sees 32 seals. Then he sees 10 more. How many seals does he see in all?

   __42__ seals

2. There are 58 birds. Then 10 fly away. How many birds are left?

   _____ birds

3. Maddie has 25 treats. She eats 10 treats. How many treats are left?

   _____ treats

4. Tosha digs 12 holes. Then she digs 10 more. How many holes does she dig in all?

   _____ holes

5. Zydie sleeps 25 minutes. Then she sleeps 10 more minutes. How many minutes does she sleep?

   _____ minutes

6. Loki has 51 pennies. Then he loses 10 pennies. How many pennies are left?

   _____ pennies

Mark the correct answer.

7. Count on by tens. Which number comes next?

   11, 21, 31, 41, _____

   ○ 40
   ○ 42
   ○ 50
   ○ 51

8. Count back by tens. Which number comes next?

   83, 73, 63, 53, _____

   ○ 43
   ○ 50
   ○ 52
   ○ 54

Reading Strategy • Make Predictions

Making predictions can help you solve problems.

Mrs. Green knits numbers on the team's ski hats.
Look for a pattern. What are the missing numbers?
What is the rule for the pattern?

27   30   36

1. Look at the numbers on the caps.
   Look for a pattern.

2. Make a prediction.
   What do you think is the rule for the pattern?

   Count by ___threes___.

3. Write the missing numbers.

   27, 30, __33__, 36, __39__, __42__

4. Was your prediction right?

   ___yes___

Make a prediction. Write the missing numbers.
Write the rule for the pattern.

5. Mr. Green paints numbers on flags.

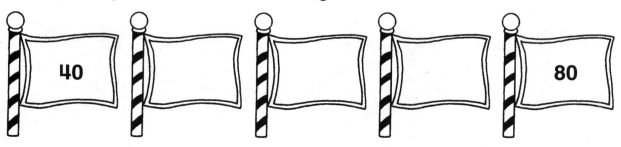

40   80

Count by _____.

Comparing Numbers

Compare the tens and ones.
Solve.

1. Beth has 17 pennies. Bob
has 23 pennies. Who has
more pennies?

_____Bob_____

2. There are 36 red balls and
26 green balls. Are there
more red balls or green
balls?

_____ balls

3. Anna has 15 pennies.
Frank has 51 pennies.
Which number of pennies
is less?

_____ pennies

4. There are 29 blue
balls.There are 92 yellow
balls. Are there fewer blue
balls or yellow balls?

_____ balls

5. Lee has 42 pennies.
Russell has 48 pennies.
Which number of pennies
is less?

_____ pennies

6. There are 54 white balls.
There are 55 red balls.
Are there more white balls
or red balls?

_____ balls

Mark the correct answer.

7. Which toy costs more?

○ truck   ○ car

8. Which toy costs less?

○ ball   ○ top

Name _____

Greater Than and Less Than

kite 12¢

ball 30¢

horn 42¢

drum 24¢

Solve.

1. Tom buys a toy. The price of the toy is greater than 35¢. Which toy does he buy?

horn

2. Jessie buys a toy. The price of the toy is less than 15¢. Which toy does she buy?

_____

3. Matt buys a toy. The price of the toy is greater than 25¢ and less than 35¢. Which toy does he buy?

_____

4. Becky buys a toy. The price of the toy is greater than 20¢ and less than 25¢. Which toy does she buy?

_____

Mark the correct answer.

5. Choose > or <.

27 ◯ 19

◯ <

◯ >

6. Choose > or <.

46 ◯ 64

◯ <

◯ >

After, Before, Between

Solve.

1. The house between 54 and 56 is missing its number. What is the house number?

<u>55</u>

2. Jason lives in the house just before 54. What is his house number?

_____

3. Marcy's house number is an odd number. What is her house number?

_____

4. Lisa's house number is 54. Wayne's is 56. Which house number is greater?

_____

Mark the correct answer.

5. Which number is just before 32?

_____, 32

○ 21

○ 22

○ 31

○ 33

6. Which number is between 15 and 17?

15, _____, 17

○ 14

○ 16

○ 18

○ 60

Name _____

Ordinal Numbers

| first | second | third | fourth | fifth | sixth | seventh | eighth |
| 1st | 2nd | 3rd | 4th | 5th | 6th | 7th | 8th |

Use the picture.
Circle the correct answer.

1. Which flower is fourth?

2. Which flower is 6th?

3. Look for a pattern. Which flower is next?

4. Is the number of flowers odd or even?

odd   even

Mark the correct answer.

5. In which position is the ◯ ?

△ ▢ ◯ ☆
first

○ first
○ second
○ third
○ fourth

6. In which position is the ☆ ?

△ ▢ ◯ ☆
first

○ 1st
○ 2nd
○ 3rd
○ 4th

Reading Strategy • Use Graphic Aids

Using number lines can help you solve problems.

Rob has 34 pennies.
- Is 34 closer to 30 or 40?
- About how many pennies does Rob have?

1. Use a number line. Find the number of pennies Rob has.

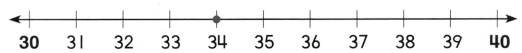

2. Count the spaces from 34 back to 30.

   __4__ spaces

3. Count the spaces from 34 on to 40.

   __6__ spaces

4. Solve the problem.

   34 is closer to __30__.

   Rob has about __30__ pennies.

Use the number line to solve.

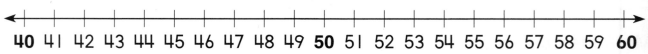

5. Joshua has 42 marbles.
   - Is 42 closer to 40 or 50?   _____
   - About how many marbles does
     Joshua have?   about _____ marbles

6. Crystal has 56 jacks.
   - Is 56 closer to 50 or 60?   _____
   - About how many jacks does
     Crystal have?   about _____ jacks

Pennies, Nickels, and Dimes

Count on to find the total amount.
Write the name of the toy you can buy.

24¢ bear

18¢ lion

37¢ frog

30¢ mouse

1.

bear _____

2.

_____

3.

_____

Mark the correct answer.

4. Which is the total amount?

○ 7¢   ○ 8¢
○ 12¢   ○ 13¢

5. Which is the total amount?

○ 7¢   ○ 12¢
○ 17¢   ○ 22¢

Nickels, Dimes, and Quarters

Draw coins to solve.

1. Alex has 1 quarter, 1 nickel, and 4 pennies.
How much money does he have?

_34_ ¢

---

2. Brian has 3 dimes and 1 nickel.
How much money does he have?

_____ ¢

---

3. Christy has 1 quarter, 2 dimes, and 2 pennies.
How much money does she have?

_____ ¢

Mark the correct answer.

4. Which is the total amount?

○ 29¢   ○ 41¢
○ 56¢   ○ 39¢

5. Which is the total amount?

○ 27¢   ○ 35¢
○ 42¢   ○ 32¢

Name _____

Counting Collections

Draw and label the coins in order from greatest to least value.
Write the total amount.

1.

___46___ ¢

2.

_____ ¢

3.

_____ ¢

Mark the correct answer.

4. Which is the total amount?

○ 36¢   ○ 41¢

○ 46¢   ○ 51¢

5. Which is the total amount?

  (image)

○ 20¢   ○ 17¢

○ 22¢   ○ 16¢

Counting Half-Dollars

Draw a picture to solve.

1. Wayne has 1 half-dollar, 3 nickels, and 2 pennies.
How much money does he have?

_67_ ¢

2. Amy has 1 quarter and 4 nickels.
How much money does she have?

_____ ¢

3. Leon has 1 half-dollar, 1 quarter, and 4 pennies.
How much money does he have?

_____ ¢

Mark the correct answer.

4. Which is the total amount?

○ 95¢   ○ 90¢

○ 85¢   ○ not here

5. Which is the total amount?

○ 71¢   ○ 66¢

○ 61¢   ○ not here

Reading Strategy • Use Pictures

Cindy buys a ball
that costs 58¢.
She uses the
fewest coins.
What coins
does she use?

1. Look at the picture.
   What coins does Cindy have?

   __1__ quarter, __3__ dimes, __3__ nickels, __4__ pennies

2. Choose the fewest coins that add up to the price of the ball.

   __1__ quarter, __2__ dimes, __2__ nickels, __3__ pennies = 58¢

Solve.

3.

   Sarah buys jacks that cost 47¢.
   She uses the fewest coins.
   How many of each coin does she use?

   _____ quarter   _____ dimes   _____ nickels   _____ pennies

---

4. Dave buys a book that costs 96¢.
   He uses the fewest coins.
   How many of each coin does he use?

   _____ half-dollar   _____ quarter   _____ dimes   _____ penny

Combinations of Coins

Draw and label the coins.
Write the amount.

1. Greg has 15¢. His father gives him 30¢. How much money does Greg have now?

___45___ ¢

2. Judy has 40¢. She earns 50¢ raking leaves. How much money does she have now?

_____ ¢

3. Bob has 1 quarter, 2 dimes, and 4 pennies. How much money does he have?

_____ ¢

Mark the correct answer.

4. Which is the total amount?

◯ 40¢

◯ 35¢

◯ 55¢

◯ 31¢

Equal Amounts Using Fewest Coins

Draw and label the coins.
Solve.

1. Allen has 1 quarter, 3 nickels, and 5 pennies. How much money does he have?

_**45**_ ¢

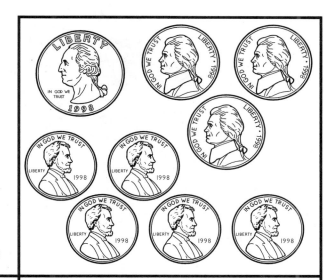

2. Paul has 4 dimes and 4 nickels. How much money does he have?

_____ ¢

Mark the correct answer.

3. Which is the total amount?

○ 30¢
○ 50¢
○ 35¢
○ 26¢

4. Which is the total amount?

○ 46¢
○ 55¢
○ 40¢
○ 45¢

PROBLEM SOLVING   PS45

Comparing Amounts

Write the names and prices of
two toys each child could buy.

1. Sally has 65¢.

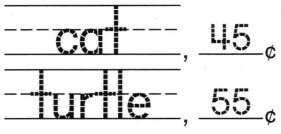

cat , 45 ¢

turtle , 55 ¢

2. Alex has 95¢.

_____ , ___ ¢

_____ , ___ ¢

3. Terry has 80¢.

_____ , ___ ¢

_____ , ___ ¢

4. James has 75¢.

_____ , ___ ¢

_____ , ___ ¢

Mark the correct answer.

5. Brad has

Does he have enough to
buy a toy that costs 60¢?

◯ yes   ◯ no

Making Change

Use coins to solve.

1. Jake has 40¢. He buys apple juice for 37¢. How much change does he get?

_____3_____ ¢

2. Kelly has 81¢. She buys a muffin for 79¢. How much change does she get?

_____ ¢

3. Kay has 2 quarters, 2 nickels, and 6 pennies. Does she have enough money to buy a doll for 65¢?

Yes   No

4. Gino has 1 half-dollar, 1 quarter, 1 dime, and 1 nickel. How much money does he have?

_____ ¢

5. Les has 3 quarters, 1 dime, and 4 pennies. How much money does he have?

_____ ¢

6. Julie has 3 dimes, 4 nickels, and 5 pennies. How much money does she have?

_____ ¢

Mark the correct answer.

7. You have 46¢.
You buy a car for 42¢.
Your change is _____.

○ 2¢
○ 3¢
○ 4¢
○ 5¢

8. You have 72¢.
You buy a ball for 69¢.
Your change is _____.

○ 2¢
○ 3¢
○ 4¢
○ 5¢

Reading Strategy • Use Word Clues

Looking for **word clues**
can help you read and
solve problems.

Tracey has 4 dimes, 2 nickels, and 3 pennies.
How much money does she have? Does she
have enough money to buy the car?

1. Draw the coins to find the total amount.

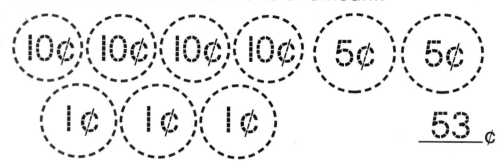

53 ¢

2. The words **does she have enough**
tell you to compare.

53 < 55

3. Does Tracey have enough money
to buy the car?

no

Use coins. Solve.
Then circle **yes** or **no**.

4. Howard has 3 dimes, 3
nickels, and 4 pennies. How
much money does he have?

_____¢

Does he have enough
money to buy the bike?

yes   no

5. Patti has 7 pennies, 1 dime,
1 nickel, and 1 quarter. How
much money does she have?

_____¢

Does she have enough
money to buy the train?

yes   no

Hour and Half-Hour

Use the picture to answer the questions.

1. What time does the
store open?

_**10:00**_

2. What time does the
store close?

_____

3. Anna has 1 half-dollar, 3
dimes, and a nickel. How
much money does Anna
have?

_____¢

4. Mark has 95¢. He spends
75¢. How much money does
he have left?

_____¢

Mark the correct answer.

5. When does the store open?

○ 4:30

○ 6:30

○ 8:30

6. When does the store close?

○ 12:30

○ 10:30

○ 6:00

PROBLEM SOLVING PS49

Telling Time to 5 Minutes

Photo Times	
Alex	9:15
Greg	9:20
Linda	9:25
Margie	9:30

Use the picture to answer the questions.

1. What time will Greg have his photo taken?

_____9:20_____

2. What time will Linda have her photo taken?

_____

3. Amy will have her photo taken 5 minutes after Margie. What time will she have her photo taken?

_____

4. Who will have a photo taken at the time shown on this clock?

_____

Mark the correct answer.

5. Which clock shows 7:25?

◯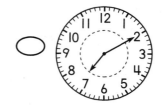

◯

6. Which clock shows 2:40?

◯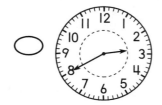

◯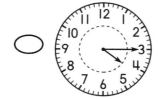

Telling Time to 15 Minutes

Write the time.

1. What time does Stan come home?

2. What time is it?

_____

3. What time does soccer practice start?

_____

4. What time does the play end?

_____

Mark the correct answer.

5. Which time does the clock show?

○ 3:50

○ 4:00

○ 11:15

6. Which time does the clock show?

○ 3:45

○ 4:45

○ 9:15

PROBLEM SOLVING PS51

Practice Telling Time

Write the time.

1. What time did Julie mail her letter?

4:05
_____

2. What time did Lee sharpen his pencil?

_____

3. What time did Kim empty the trash?

_____

4. What time did Brian leave?

_____

Mark the correct answer.

5. How long does it take you to write your telephone number?

○ about 1 second

○ about 1 minute

○ about 1 hour

6. How long would it take you to write a 1-page story?

○ about 1 second

○ about 1 minute

○ about 1 hour

Reading Strategy • Use Word Clues

Read the problem.
Look for word clues.

Use the clocks.
Draw the hands to
show the time.

Band practice **starts** at 3:00.
It **lasts** for **1 hour.**
What **time** is band
practice **over**?

Band practice is over at _____ 4:00 _____.

Look for word clues. Use the clocks to solve.

1. The band concert starts at 7:30.
   It lasts for 2 hours. What time is
   the band concert over?

_____

2. Roger goes to a friend's house
   at 4:00. He comes home 1 hour
   later. What time does Roger
   come home?

_____

3. Kora starts playing at 3:00.
   She plays for 30 minutes.
   What time does she stop
   playing?

_____

4. Ben starts his homework at
   5:30. It takes him 35 minutes.
   What time does he finish his
   homework?

_____

Reading a Calendar

Use the calendar to answer the questions.

May

Sunday	Monday	Tuesday	Wednesday	Thursday	Friday	Saturday
					1	2
3	4	5	6	7	8	9
Mother's Day 10	11	12	13	14	15	16
17	18	19	20	21	22	23
24	25	26	27	28	29	30
31						

1. On which day does the month start?

___Friday___

2. What is the day and date of Mother's Day?

_____ , _____

3. What is the date of the fourth Friday?

_____

Use the calendar.
Mark the correct answer.

4. Which is the date of the third Tuesday?

○ May 12

○ May 13

○ May 19

○ May 20

5. On which day does the month end?

○ Saturday

○ Sunday

○ Monday

○ Tuesday

Using a Calendar

Use the calendar to answer the questions.

January	February	March	April
Su M T W Th F Sa	Su M T W Th F Sa	Su M T W Th F Sa	Su M T W Th F Sa
1 2 3	1 2 3 4 5 6 7	1 2 3 4 5 6 7	1 2 3 4
4 5 6 7 8 9 10	8 9 10 11 12 13 14	8 9 10 11 12 13 14	5 6 7 8 9 10 11
11 12 13 14 15 16 17	15 16 17 18 19 20 21	15 16 17 18 19 20 21	12 13 14 15 16 17 18
18 19 20 21 22 23 24	22 23 24 25 26 27 28	22 23 24 25 26 27 28	19 20 21 22 23 24 25
25 26 27 28 29 30 31		29 30 31	26 27 27 29 30

May	June	July	August
Su M T W Th F Sa	Su M T W Th F Sa	Su M T W Th F Sa	Su M T W Th F Sa
1 2	1 2 3 4 5 6	1 2 3 4	1
3 4 5 6 7 8 9	7 8 9 10 11 12 13	5 6 7 8 9 10 11	2 3 4 5 6 7 8
10 11 12 13 14 15 16	14 15 16 17 18 19 20	12 13 14 15 16 17 18	9 10 11 12 13 14 15
17 18 19 20 21 22 23	21 22 23 24 25 26 27	19 20 21 22 23 24 25	16 17 18 19 20 21 22
24 25 26 27 28 29 30	28 29 30	26 27 28 29 30 31	23 24 25 26 27 28 29
31			30 31

September	October	November	December
Su M T W Th F Sa	Su M T W Th F Sa	Su M T W Th F Sa	Su M T W Th F Sa
1 2 3 4 5	1 2 3	1 2 3 4 5 6 7	1 2 3 4 5
6 7 8 9 10 11 12	4 5 6 7 8 9 10	8 9 10 11 12 13 14	6 7 8 9 10 11 12
13 14 15 16 17 18 19	11 12 13 14 15 16 17	15 16 17 18 19 20 21	13 14 15 16 17 18 19
20 21 22 23 24 25 26	18 19 20 21 22 23 24	22 23 24 25 26 27 28	20 21 22 23 24 25 26
27 28 29 30	25 26 27 28 29 30 31	29 30	27 28 29 30 31

1. Which month follows May?

June

2. Which is the ninth month in the year?

_____

3. Gale leaves April 11. She comes home 1 week later. On what date does she come home?

_____

Use the calendar.
Mark the correct answer.

4. Which month follows March?

◯ April   ◯ July

◯ August   ◯ not here

5. Which date follows April 30?

◯ April 30   ◯ April 31

◯ May 1   ◯ not here

Early or Late

Write each time. Write **early** or **late**.

1. School starts at  . _____ 8:30

Rob gets there at  . _____ 8:15

Is Rob early or late? _____ early

2. The game starts at  . _____

Leslie gets there at  . _____

Is Leslie early or late? _____

Mark the correct answer.

3. The movie starts at .

Ron gets there at .

Is Ron early or late?

○ early   ○ late

4. The picnic starts at 2:00. Grace gets there at 2:15. Is she early or late?

○ early

○ late

Sequencing Events

Erika made a birthday card for her mom.
Number the events in order.
Write the time of each event.

1. Erika signed her name to the card at  .

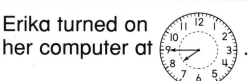

___4___ , ___8:30___

Erika printed the card at .

_____ , _____

Erika turned on her computer at  .

_____ , _____

Erika typed HAPPY BIRTHDAY MOM at .

_____ , _____

2. Erika gave her mom the card at

 .

_____ , _____

Erika and her mom ate birthday cake at

 .

_____ , _____

Erika's mom came home at

 .

_____ , _____

Mark the correct answer.

3. What time is it?

○ 1:00
○ 7:05
○ 5:15
○ 1:55

4. What time is it?

○ 2:25
○ 12:25
○ 2:55
○ 5:30

Reading Strategy • Use Graphic Aids

Using schedules can help you solve problems.

Marlo's class went on a field trip to the park. How long does it take to get to the park?

Field Trip Schedule	
9:30 – 10:00	Go to park.
10:00 – 11:30	Tour park.
11:30 – 12:30	Eat lunch.
12:30 – 1:00	Go back to school.

1. When does Marlo's class leave for the park? __9:30__

2. When does Marlo's class get to the park? __10:00__

3. Solve the problem.

   It takes __30__ minutes to get to the park.

Use the schedule to answer the questions.

4. How long does Marlo's class spend touring the park?

   _____ hour _____ minutes

5. What time does Marlo's class finish eating lunch?

   _____

6. How much time passes from the time Marlo's class gets to the park to the time Marlo's class leaves the park?

   _____ hours _____ minutes

7. How much time passes from the time Marlo's class leaves school to the time Marlo's class gets back to school?

   _____ hours _____ minutes

Regrouping Ones as Tens

Use Workmat 3 and ⬚⬚⬚⬚⬚⬚⬚⬚ ▱.
Add. Write how many tens and ones.

1. John has 7 white beads.
   He has 7 yellow beads.
   How many beads does
   he have?

   __14__ beads

   __1__ ten __4__ ones

2. Michele has 6 bird stickers.
   She has 5 cat stickers.
   How many stickers does
   she have?

   _____ stickers

   _____ ten _____ one

3. Megan has 5 yellow balls.
   She has 8 green balls.
   How many balls does
   she have?

   _____ balls

   _____ ten _____ ones

4. Cecil has 9 red train cars.
   He has 8 blue train cars.
   How many train cars does
   he have?

   _____ train cars

   _____ ten _____ ones

Mark the correct answer.

5. Can you make a ten?

   $9 + 7 =$ _____

   ○ yes

   ○ no

6. Can you make a ten?

   $3 + 4 =$ _____

   ○ yes

   ○ no

Modeling One-Digit and Two-Digit Addition

Use Workmat 3 and ⬜⬜⬜⬜⬜⬜⬜⬜⬜ ⬜.
Add.

1. Ben made 13 plain muffins and 9 raisin muffins. How many muffins did he make?

_22_ muffins

2. It took 15 minutes to make cookies. It took 7 minutes to clean up. How many minutes did it take in all?

_____ minutes

3. Mrs. Lewis used 7 apples for one pie. She used 6 apples for another pie. How many apples did she use?

_____ apples

4. Mr. Davis made 5 loaves of white bread and 6 loaves of wheat bread. How many loaves of bread did he make?

_____ loaves of bread

Mark the correct answer.

5. Maria has 13 pretzels. Amy gives her 8 more. How many pretzels does Maria have now?

○ 11

○ 21

○ 5

○ 15

6. Tosha has 11 pencils. Mr. Loki gives her 5 more. How many pencils does Tosha have now?

○ 12

○ 26

○ 6

○ 16

Modeling Two-Digit Addition

Use Workmat 3 and ⬚⬚⬚⬚⬚⬚⬚⬚ ⬚.
Add.

1. Paul sees 18 deer on Monday. He sees 9 deer on Tuesday. How many deer does he see on both days together?

_27_ deer

2. Chuck sees 16 deer on Tuesday. He sees 21 deer on Wednesday. How many deer does he see on both days together?

_____ deer

3. Julie sees 15 deer on Wednesday. She sees 7 deer on Thursday. How many deer does she see on both days together?

_____ deer

4. Natalie sees 12 deer on Thursday. She sees 19 deer on Friday. How many deer does she see on both days together?

_____ deer

Mark the correct answer.

5. Jen sees 13 deer on Saturday and 18 deer on Sunday. How many deer does she see in all?

○ 21
○ 25
○ 31
○ 35

6. Jon sees 9 deer on Monday and 13 deer on Tuesday. How many deer does he see in all?

○ 22
○ 24
○ 29
○ 32

Recording Two-Digit Addition

Use Workmat 3 and ▭▭▭▭▭▭▭▭▭ ▢.
Add.

1. There are 22 people on a bus. There are 20 people on another bus. How many people in all?

_42_ people

2. There are 17 people on a bus. There are 15 people on another bus. How many people in all?

_____ people

3. There are 29 adults at the soccer game. There are 34 children. How many people are there in all?

_____ people

4. There are 16 boy soccer players. There are 19 girl soccer players. How many players are there in all?

_____ players

Mark the correct answer.

5. There are 53 birds in the trees. There are 14 birds on the grass. How many birds are there in all?

○ 57
○ 59
○ 67
○ 69

6. There are 46 blue marbles. There are 25 green marbles. How many marbles are there in all?

○ 69
○ 71
○ 73
○ 61

Reading Strategy • Visualize

Picturing a problem in your mind
can help you solve the problem.

During the year, Kira reads 15
books about animals and 17
adventure books. How many
books does Kira read in all?

1. Read the problem.
   Picture the books that Kira reads.

2. Think about how to model the
   problem using ⬚⬚⬚⬚⬚⬚⬚⬚ ▢.

3. Use ⬚⬚⬚⬚⬚⬚⬚⬚ ▢.
   Add. Regroup if you need to.

tens	ones
1	5
+ 1	7
3	2

4. Solve the problem.

   Kira reads __32__ books in all.

Picture the problem.
Use ⬚⬚⬚⬚⬚⬚⬚⬚ ▢ to solve.

5. Kenny reads 22 mysteries
   and 18 riddle books. How
   many books does he read
   in all?

tens	ones
2	2
+ 1	8

   _____ books

Adding One-Digit and Two-Digit Numbers

Use Workmat 3 and ⬚⬚⬚⬚⬚⬚⬚ ⬚.

Solve.

1. Roy picked 58 berries. Then he picked 5 more. How many berries did he pick in all? _____**63**_____ berries	$\begin{array}{r} \overset{1}{5}8 \\ +5 \\ \hline 63 \end{array}$
2. Paula had 66 toy animals. She got 4 more for her birthday. How many animals does she have now? _____ animals	
3. Allison had 15 rocks. She found 3 more. How many rocks does she have now? _____ rocks	

Mark the correct answer.

4. Victor planted 47 pea seeds. He planted 8 bean seeds. How many seeds did he plant in all?

○ 55

○ 56

○ 65

5. It took Angela 16 minutes to do math. It took her 8 minutes to do spelling. How long did it take for both?

○ 24 minutes

○ 22 minutes

○ 14 minutes

Adding Two-Digit Numbers

Solve.

1. Alice read 25 pages of her book before lunch. After lunch, she read 12 pages. How many pages did she read in all?

__37__ pages

$$\begin{array}{r} 25 \\ +12 \\ \hline 37 \end{array}$$

2. Troy read a book with 36 pages last week. This week he read a book with 27 pages. How many pages did he read in all?

_____ pages

3. William read 8 pages of his book on Monday. On Tuesday, he read twice as many pages. How many pages did he read in all?

_____ pages

Mark the correct answer.

4. Ned read two books. One had 48 pages. The other had 16 pages. How many pages did he read?

○ 54   ○ 56
○ 62   ○ 64

5. Eve read two books. Each book had 42 pages. How many pages did she read?

○ 44   ○ 66
○ 84   ○ 88

More About Two-Digit Addition

Solve.

1. Laura had 57¢. She found 25¢ on the sidewalk. How much money does she have now?

    _82_ ¢

$$\begin{array}{r} \overset{1}{5}7 \\ +25 \\ \hline 82 \end{array}$$

2. Nathan saved 65¢. This week he will save 5¢. How much money will he have then?

    _____ ¢

3. Carol has 72 pennies in a bowl. She has 7 pennies in her pocket. How much money does she have in all?

    _____ ¢

Mark the best answer.

4. The band members sold 46 large shirts and 29 extra-large shirts. How many shirts did they sell in all?

    ○ 56   ○ 65

    ○ 75   ○ 76

5. The band members sold 38 white caps and 50 blue caps. How many caps did they sell in all?

    ○ 43   ○ 58

    ○ 85   ○ 88

Addition Practice

	Girls	Boys
Grade 2	35	45
Grade 3	41	28

Use the chart to answer the questions.

1. How many children are in Grade 2?

__80__ children

2. How many boys are there in the two grades?

_____ boys

3. How many girls are there in the two grades?

_____ girls

4. How many children are in Grade 3?

_____ children

Mark the correct answer.

5. There are 26 girls and 29 boys in Grade 5. How many children are there in all?

○ 45

○ 55

○ 65

6. There are 36 boys and 40 girls in Grade 1. How many children are there in Grade 1?

○ 40

○ 76

○ 86

Reading Strategy • Noting Details

Reading for details can help you solve problems.

Nicole buys 24 lion stamps and 38 tiger stamps. She buys 14 postcards. How many stamps does Nicole buy?

1. Read the problem.
   What information do you need
   to solve the problem? Circle it.

2. What information is not needed?
   Draw a line through that sentence.

3. Solve the problem.

   Nicole buys __62__ stamps.

$$\begin{array}{r} \overset{1}{2}4 \\ +38 \\ \hline 62 \end{array}$$

Draw a line through the sentence that
is not needed. Then solve.

4. Toby reads 32 pages about gorillas
   and 48 pages about rhinos. Jack
   reads 26 pages about elephants.
   How many pages does Toby read?

   _____ pages

5. Mr. Lewis takes 23 pictures on
   Tuesday and 29 pictures on
   Wednesday. Mrs. Lewis takes 36
   pictures on both days. How many
   pictures does Mr. Lewis take on
   Monday and Tuesday together?

   _____ pictures

Regrouping Tens as Ones

Use Workmat 3 and ▭▭▭▭▭▭▭ ▭ .

Subtract. Write how many tens
and ones are left.

1. There are 17 people
sledding. Then 9 people
go home. How many
are left?

__8__ people

__0__ tens __8__ ones

2. There are 23 people sledding.
There are 5 people skating.
How many more people are
sledding than skating?

_____ more people

_____ ten _____ ones

3. There are 22 boys skating.
There are 7 girls skating.
How many more boys than
girls are skating?

_____ more boys

_____ ten _____ ones

4. There are 30 people making
snow forts. Then 8 go home.
How many people are left?

_____ people

_____ tens _____ ones

Mark the correct answer.

5. There are 38 children at the
game. Then 6 go home.
How many children are left?

○ 22   ○ 26

○ 32   ○ 44

6. There are 24 red balloons.
There are 8 blue balloons.
How many more red balloons
than blue balloons are there?

○ 32   ○ 26

○ 22   ○ 16

Modeling One-Digit and Two-Digit Subtraction

Use Workmat 3 and ⬚⬚⬚⬚⬚⬚⬚⬚ ⬚.

Subtract.

1. There are 24 children in a play. 8 children dance. The other children sing. How many children sing?

___16___ children

2. There are 30 chairs at the play. There are 5 couches. How many more chairs than couches are there?

_____ more chairs

3. Hannah sold 21 tickets for the play. Anna sold 7 tickets. How many more tickets did Hannah sell than Anna?

_____ more tickets

4. On Friday, 44 people came to the play. On Saturday, 4 fewer people came. How many came on Saturday?

_____ people

Mark the correct answer.

5. There are 25 girls and 9 boys in the play. How many more girls than boys are in the play?

○ 34

○ 26

○ 16

○ 14

6. Yolanda sold 29 adult tickets and 8 student tickets. How many more adult tickets than student tickets did she sell?

○ 37

○ 31

○ 27

○ 21

Recording Subtraction

Use Workmat 3 and ▭▭▭▭▭▭▭▭▭ ▫.

Subtract.

1. There are 36 airplanes at an airport. Then 5 fly away. How many are left?

_31_ airplanes

2. There are 24 airplanes. 8 are jets. How many are not jets?

_____ airplanes

3. There are 31 airplanes on the ground. There are 6 fewer airplanes in the air. How many are in the air?

_____ airplanes

4. There are 20 adults and 5 children on the airplane. How many more adults than children are there?

_____ more adults

Mark the correct answer.

5. Nick has 42 model airplanes. He gives 6 to Amber. How many does he have left?

- ○ 48
- ○ 46
- ○ 38
- ○ 36

6. Maya has 28 grapes. Susan has 5. How many more grapes does Maya have than Susan?

- ○ 33
- ○ 25
- ○ 23
- ○ 18

Recording Two-Digit Subtraction

Use Workmat 3 and ⬚⬚⬚⬚⬚⬚⬚⬚⬚⬚ ⬚.

Find the difference.

1. There are 38 geese and 24 ducks at a pond. How many more geese than ducks are there?

_**14**_ more geese

2. There are 41 seagulls on the beach. Then 7 fly away. How many are left?

_____ seagulls

3. There are 27 birds on a wire. 8 of the birds are singing. How many are not singing?

_____ birds

4. Kirk sees 30 blue jays. He sees 18 robins. How many more blue jays than robins does he see?

_____ more blue jays

Mark the correct answer.

5. Harry has 45 stamps. He gives 13 to Julie. How many stamps does he have left?

○ 22
○ 32
○ 38
○ 42

6. There are 31 birds at a feeder. There are 12 at the bird bath. How many more are at the feeder than at the bird bath?

○ 29
○ 23
○ 19
○ 13

Reading Strategy • Use Word Clues

Using word clues can help you solve problems.

Rich spends 37¢ to buy a pretzel and 39¢ to buy lemonade. How much money does Rich spend in all?	Lois has 82¢ in her pocket. She spends 48¢ on juice. How much money does she have left?

1. Read the problems. Look for word clues.

The words **spends 37¢, and 39¢, in all** tell you to add.
The words **has 82¢, spends 48¢, have left** tell you to subtract.

2. Add or subtract. Solve.

tens	ones
I	
3	7
+3	9
7	6

Rich spends __76__ ¢ in all.

tens	ones
7	12
8̸	2̸
—4	8
3	4

Lois has __34__ ¢ left.

Look for word clues.
Find the sum or difference.

3. Renee's mom gives her 75¢. Renee buys an apple for 59¢. How much money does Renee have left?

_____ ¢

4. Chris buys a cookie for 17¢. Then he buys juice for 45¢. How much money does Chris spend in all?

_____ ¢

Subtracting One-Digit from Two-Digit Numbers

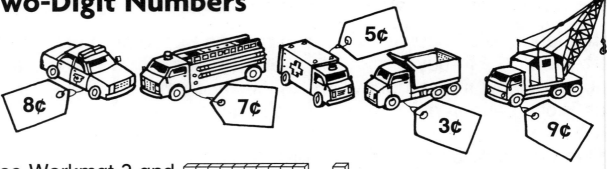

Use Workmat 3 and ▭▭▭▭▭▭▭▭ ▢.
Solve.

I. Les had 42¢. He bought a
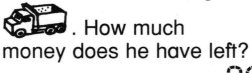. How much
money does he have left?

_____39_____ ¢

$$\begin{array}{r} \overset{3}{\cancel{4}}\overset{12}{\cancel{2}} \\ -\quad 3 \\ \hline 39 \end{array}$$

2. Grace had 50¢. She bought
a 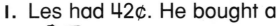. How much
money does she have now?

_____ ¢

3. Aaron has 36¢. How much
will he have left if he buys

a  ?

_____ ¢

Mark the correct answer.

4. Greg has 59¢. He buys a
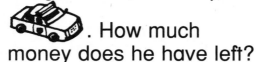. How much
money does he have left?

tens	ones
5	9
−	8

○ 41¢

○ 51¢

○ 67¢

Two-Digit Subtraction

Use Workmat 3 and  .
Solve.

1. On Saturday morning 32 cars and 15 vans came to the car wash. How many more cars than vans came?

_____17_____ more cars

$$\begin{array}{r} \overset{2\;\;12}{\cancel{3}\cancel{2}} \\ -\;1\;5 \\ \hline 1\;7 \end{array}$$

2. Ms. West has 46¢. How many cents more does she need for a car wash?

_____¢

3. 32 cars were washed in the morning. 27 were washed in the afternoon. How many cars were washed in all?

_____cars

Mark the correct answer.

4. One day 45 cars and 19 trucks were washed. How many more cars than trucks were washed?

tens	ones
4	5
− 1	9

○ 36
○ 34
○ 26
○ 24

Practicing Two-Digit Subtraction

Solve.

1. Megan had 73 books at the garage sale. She sold 42. How many are left? ___31___ books	$\begin{array}{r} 73 \\ -\,42 \\ \hline 31 \end{array}$
2. Wayne had 50¢. He bought a shirt for 35¢. How much money did he have left? _____¢	
3. There were 24 garden tools for sale. Brenda bought 10. How many were left? _____ garden tools	

Mark the correct answer.

4. Cal had 32 toys for sale. He sold 16. How many were left?

tens	ones
3	2
− 1	6

○ 14
○ 16
○ 24
○ 26

Using Addition to Check Subtraction

Subtract.
Add to check.

1. Devin cut out 75 snowflakes and 44 stars. How many more snowflakes did he cut out? __37__ more snowflakes	$\begin{array}{r} 75 \\ -\ 44 \\ \hline 31 \end{array}$
2. Zach made 61 moons. Jan made 9 moons. How many more moons did Zach make? _____ more moons	
3. Lana wants 84 stars. She has made 37. How many more stars must she make? _____ more stars	

Mark the correct answer.

4. Which numbers should you add to check the subtraction problem?

$\begin{array}{r} 57 \\ -\ 25 \\ \hline 32 \end{array}$

◯ $\begin{array}{r} 32 \\ +\ 25 \end{array}$ ◯ $\begin{array}{r} 57 \\ +\ 25 \end{array}$

◯ $\begin{array}{r} 32 \\ +\ 57 \end{array}$ ◯ $\begin{array}{r} 32 \\ +\ 32 \end{array}$

Reading Strategy • Use Pictures

Using pictures can help you solve problems.

Lorna has 86¢.

She buys a ⬭.

How much money
does she have left?

39¢

28¢

Ann buys a ⬭ and a
⚷ . How much money
does she need?

1. Read the problems. Look at the picture.

The ⬭ costs __39__ ¢.

The ⬭ costs __39__ ¢.

The ⚷ costs __28__ ¢.

2. Add or subtract.

tens	ones
7	16
8̸	6̸
−3	9
4	7

Lorna has __47__ ¢ left.

tens	ones
1	
3	9
+2	8
6	7

Ann needs __67__ ¢.

Use the picture. Solve.

3. Sam buys a 🎵 and a ⚷ .
   How much money does he need?

62¢   28¢   _____ ¢

4. Carol has 60¢. She buys a ⬭.
   How much money does she have left?

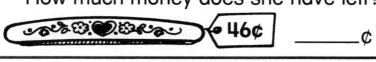

46¢   _____ ¢

Tally Tables

Use the table to answer the questions.

What Lynn Saw at the River	
frogs	IIII I
fish	III
birds	IIII
beavers	II

1. Did Lynn see more frogs
   or more birds?

   __frogs__

2. How many frogs and fish
   did Lynn see?

   _____ frogs and fish

3. How many more birds than
   beavers did Lynn see?

   _____ more birds

4. How many animals did Lynn
   see in all?

   _____ animals

Mark the correct answer.

5. How many frogs did
   Lynn see?

   ○ 3

   ○ 4

   ○ 5

   ○ 6

6. Lynn saw the greatest
   number of which animal?

   ○ frog

   ○ bird

   ○ fish

   ○ beaver

Reading Strategy • Use Graphic Aids

Using tables can help you solve problems.

The table shows the favorite kinds of books of the children in the book club. How many more children like animal books than mystery books?

Favorite Books	
mystery	||
adventure	||||
animals	|||||	
sports	|||

1. Look at the table.
Count the tally marks.

___2___ like mystery books best.

___6___ like animal books best.

2. Write a number sentence.

___6___ – ___2___ = ___4___

3. Solve the problem.

___4___ more children like animal books than mystery books.

Use the table. Solve.

4. How many kinds of books got fewer than 4 votes?

_____ kinds of books

5. How many children are in the book club?

_____ children

Taking a Survey

This table shows what a group of children learned from a survey.

How do you get to school?	
bus	ЖЖ |||
car	ЖЖ ||
bike	||||
walk	ЖЖ

Use the table to answer the questions.

1. How many children ride the bus to school?

___8___ children

2. How many children walk to school?

_____ children

3. How many more children ride the bus than ride bikes to school?

_____ more children

4. How many children answered the survey in all?

_____ children

Mark the correct answer.

5. How many children come to school in a car?

○ 4

○ 5

○ 7

6. Altogether, how many children ride the bus and ride in cars?

○ 15

○ 13

○ 12

Comparing Data in Tables

Use the tables to answer the questions.

Books read by Sue	
first week	卌 卌
second week	卌 |||
third week	卌	
fourth week	卌	

Books read by Ed	
first week	卌 卌
second week	||||
third week	卌 |||
fourth week	卌 卌	

1. Who read more books the third week?

_____Ed_____

2. During which week did Sue and Ed read the same number of books?

_____

3. During which two weeks did Sue read the same number of books?

_____

4. How many more books did Ed read the fourth week than he read the third week?

_____

Mark the correct answer.

5. In which week did Sue read twice as many books as Ed?

○ first

○ second

○ third

○ fourth

6. How many books did Sue and Ed read the first week?

○ 4

○ 5

○ 15

○ 20

Picture Graphs

Use the graph to answer the questions.

Animals at the Pet Store	
mice	🐭🐭🐭🐭🐭🐭🐭🐭🐭🐭
guinea pigs	🐹🐹🐹🐹🐹🐹
fish	🐟🐟🐟🐟🐟
hamsters	🐹🐹🐹🐹🐹🐹🐹🐹🐹

1. How many fish are at the pet store?

   ____5____ fish

2. Are there more mice or more guinea pigs?

   _____

3. The pet store has the most of which animal?

   _____

4. How many more hamsters than fish are there?

   _____ more hamsters

Mark the correct answer.

5. The pet store has fewest of which animal?

   ◯ mice

   ◯ guinea pigs

   ◯ fish

   ◯ hamsters

6. There are 9 of which animal at the pet store?

   ◯ mice

   ◯ guinea pigs

   ◯ fish

   ◯ hamsters

Pictographs

Use the pictograph to answer the questions.

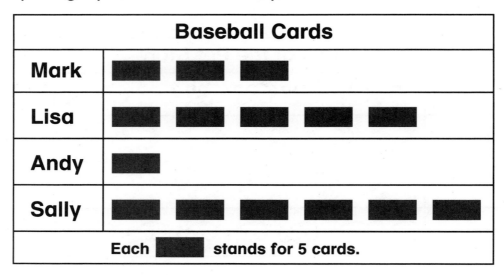

Baseball Cards						
Mark	▮	▮	▮			
Lisa	▮	▮	▮	▮	▮	
Andy	▮					
Sally	▮	▮	▮	▮	▮	▮

Each ▮ stands for 5 cards.

1. How many cards does Lisa have?

_25_ cards

2. Who has the most cards?

_____

3. How many more cards does Sally have than Mark?

_____ more cards

4. Who has the fewest cards?

_____

Mark the correct answer.

5. Who has 5 cards?

○ Mark

○ Lisa

○ Andy

○ Sally

6. Who has 5 more cards than Lisa?

○ Mark

○ Lisa

○ Andy

○ Sally

Horizontal Bar Graphs

Use the tally table to fill in the bar graph.

Number of Clocks in Our Homes	
Marla	ЖН I
Lynn	IIII
Sasha	ЖН IIII
Greg	ЖН II

Number of Clocks in Our Homes										
Marla										
Lynn										
Sasha										
Greg										

0   1   2   3   4   5   6   7   8   9   10

1. How many clocks are in Greg's home? ___7___ clocks

2. How many more clocks are in Marla's home than are in Lynn's? _____ more clocks

Mark the correct answer.

3. How many clocks are in Sasha's home?

○ 4

○ 8

○ 9

4. Who has 5 more clocks than Lynn?

○ Marla

○ Sasha

○ Greg

Reading Strategy • Use Graphic Aids

Using a graph can help you solve a problem.

Anna asks 10 classmates which sport is their favorite. She fills in the tally table to show their answers.

Favorite Sports	
baseball	||
soccer	‖‖‖
basketball	|||

Use the tally table to fill in the graph.

1. Look at the table.
   Count the tally marks.

   __2__ like baseball.

   __5__ like soccer.

   __3__ like basketball.

2. Fill in the graph.

3. Check the graph.
   Make sure it matches the table.

Favorite Sports					
baseball					
soccer					
basketball					

0 1 2 3 4 5

Use the graph. Solve.

4. How many more classmates like soccer than baseball?

   _____ more classmates

5. How many classmates in all like baseball and basketball?

   _____ classmates

Certain or Impossible

Use the tally table.
Solve.

Coins in Marsha's Bank	
quarters	ⅢⅠ Ⅰ
nickels	Ⅰ
dimes	ⅠⅠ
pennies	ⅢⅠ ⅠⅠⅠ

1. How many quarters does
Marsha have?

_____6_____ quarters

2. How many more pennies than
dimes does Marsha have?

_____ more pennies

3. Is it certain or impossible
that Marsha will find 3
quarters in her bank?

_____

4. Is it certain or impossible
that Marsha will find 3
nickels in her bank?

_____

Mark the correct answer.

5. Which coins is Marsha
certain to find in
her bank?

○ 8 dimes

○ 8 nickels

○ 8 pennies

○ 8 quarters

6. Which group of coins is
impossible to find in
Marsha's bank?

○ 2 pennies

○ 2 dimes

○ 2 nickels

○ 2 quarters

Interpreting Outcomes of Games

The table shows the outcomes of 15 spins.

Color	Tally Marks
red	~~IIII~~ IIII
blue	IIII
yellow	II

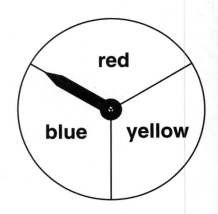

1. How many times did the pointer stop on red?

    ___9___ times

2. How many times did the pointer stop on yellow?

    _____ times

3. Which color did the pointer stop on most often?

    _____

4. Which color did the pointer stop on least often?

    _____

Mark the correct answer.

5. How many more times did the pointer stop on red than on blue?

    ○ 3
    ○ 4
    ○ 5
    ○ 6

6. How many more times did the pointer stop on blue than on yellow?

    ○ 1
    ○ 2
    ○ 3
    ○ 4

Most Likely

Carolyn pulled a blue tile from her
bag 9 times. She pulled a red tile
5 times and a yellow tile 1 time.

1. Which color did Carolyn
pull most often?

___blue___

2. Do you think there are more
red tiles or more yellow tiles
in Carolyn's bag?

_____

3. Draw a picture to show the tiles
that might be in Carolyn's bag.

Mark the correct answer.

4. There are 4 red balls in a
bag. There are 8 yellow balls
and 12 green balls in the
bag. Which color are you
most likely to pull?

◯ red

◯ yellow

◯ green

5. There are 4 circles in a bag.
There are 8 squares and 2
triangles in the bag. Which
figure are you most likely
to pull?

◯ triangle

◯ square

◯ circle

Less Likely

1. Color the tiles. Make a prediction.
Circle the bag that you think you
are less likely to pull red from.

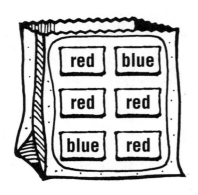
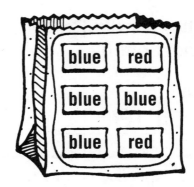

2. Put the tiles in 2 bags.
Pull out 1 tile 10 times.
Make a tally mark each time.

Color	Tally Marks
blue	
red	

Color	Tally Marks
blue	
red	

3. Was your prediction correct?   Yes   No

Mark the correct answer.

4. Which color is the spinner
less likely to stop on?

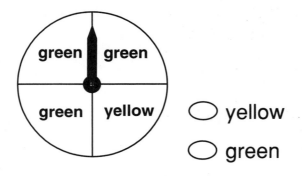

○ yellow

○ green

5. Which color is the spinner
more likely to stop on?

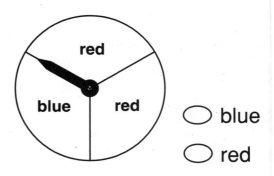

○ blue

○ red

Identifying Solids

Write the name of the solid figure.

 **rectangular prism**

 **sphere**

 **cone**

 **cylinder**

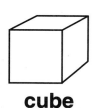 **cube**

 pyramid

1. I am a can.
I am a drum.
What solid figure am I?

cylinder

2. I hold ice cream.
I am a party hat.
What solid figure am I?

_____

3. I am a globe.
I am a beach ball.
What solid figure am I?

_____

4. I am a shoe box.
I am a book.
What solid figure am I?

_____

Mark the correct answer.

5. Which object is shaped like this solid figure?

○
○
○

6. Which object has the same shape as this solid figure?

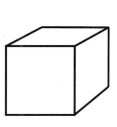
○
○
○

Sorting Solid Figures

Write the name of the solid figure.

rectangular prism

cone

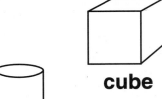
cube

pyramid

sphere

cylinder

---

1. It has 2 faces. It can roll.

_____

2. It has 5 faces. It cannot be stacked.

_____

---

3. It is sometimes a baseball. It is sometimes a grapefruit.

_____

4. It is sometimes a brick. It is sometimes a cereal box.

_____

Mark the correct answer.

5. Which solid has 6 faces and cannot roll?

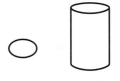

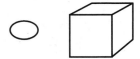

6. Which solid has 1 face and cannot be stacked?

Reading Strategy • Make Predictions

Making predictions can help you solve problems.

Lisa makes this pattern with beads.
There is a mistake in the pattern.
What mistake do you see?

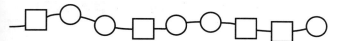

1. What is the pattern rule?

_____
square, circle, circle

2. Read Lisa's pattern.
square, circle, circle, square, circle, circle, square,?

3. Make a prediction. What comes next?

_____
circle

4. Cross out the mistake.
Draw the figure that belongs.

Find the pattern rule. Cross out the mistake.
Draw the figure that belongs.

5. Ralph makes this stamp pattern.

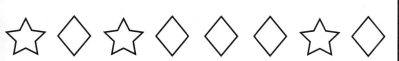

6. Fran makes this block pattern.

Making Plane Figures

  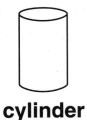 

rectangular prism   **sphere**   **cone**   **cylinder**   **cube**   **pyramid**

Write the name of the solid figure.

1. It has 6 faces that are rectangles. _____	**2.** This solid figure has 6 faces that are the same shape. _____
3. This solid figure has 2 faces that are circles. _____	**4.** This solid figure has 4 faces that are triangles. _____

Mark the correct answer.

5. Which plane figure could you trace from the solid figure?

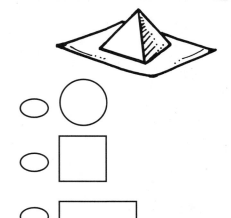

6. Which plane figure could you trace from the solid figure?

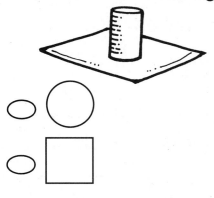

Plane Figures

Circle the correct figure.

1. Jerry is drawing a picture. He draws a circle for the sun. Which figure does he draw?

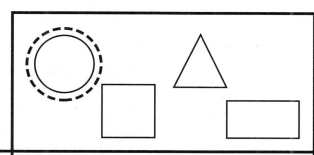

2. Meg is drawing a picture. She draws a triangle for a tree. Which figure does she draw?

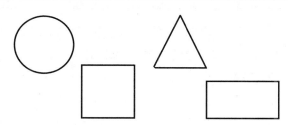

3. Marty is drawing a picture. He draws a rectangle for a truck. Which figure does he draw?

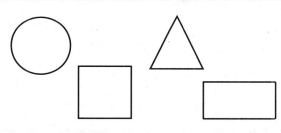

4. Lori is drawing a picture. She draws a square for a window. Which figure does she draw?

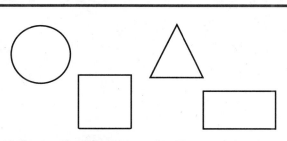

Mark the correct answer.

5. Which is a circle?

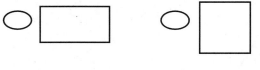

6. Which is a rectangle?

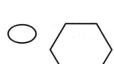

PROBLEM SOLVING PS95

Sides and Corners

Solve.

1. Les draws a figure with 3 sides and 3 corners. Draw the figure.	
2. What figure did Les draw? Write **circle, square,** or **triangle.** _____	
3. Tammy traces the solid figure. Which shape can she trace? Circle your answer. rectangle circle triangle	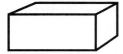
4. Craig draws a figure with 0 sides and 0 corners. Draw the figure.	

Mark the correct answer.

5. How many corners?

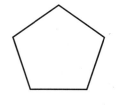

◯ 3
◯ 4
◯ 5
◯ 6

6. How many sides?

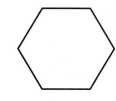

◯ 3
◯ 4
◯ 5
◯ 6

Separating to Make New Figures

Solve.

1. Jennifer has a ring.
The ring is shaped like a circle.
Circle the shape of her ring.

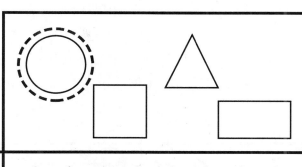

2. Dave draws a square. Kevin
draws a line on it to make
2 triangles. What line does
Kevin draw?

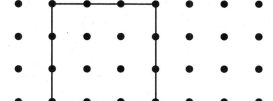

3. Steve draws a rectangle.
Lucy draws lines on it to
make 4 smaller rectangles.
What lines does Lucy draw?

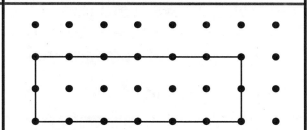

4. Tim draws a figure with 4
sides and 4 corners. Draw
the figure.

Mark the correct answer.

5. Trace the line. Which figures
did you make?

○ rectangles

○ triangles

○ squares

6. Trace the line. Which figures
did you make?

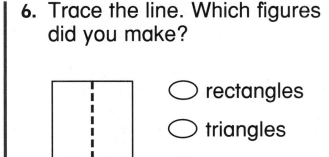

○ rectangles

○ triangles

○ squares

Congruent Figures

Write the answer.

1. Hank has 2 squares of paper that are the same shape. The 2 squares are not the same size. Are they congruent?

   ___no___

2. Michael draws a rectangle. Circle the figure he draws.

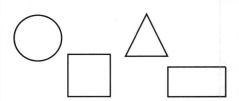

3. Annette draws two kites. The kites are the same size and shape. Are they congruent?

   Yes   No

4. How many sides and corners does each of Annette's kites have?

   _____ sides, _____ corners

Mark the correct answer.

5. Are the figures the same size and shape?

   ○ yes

   ○ no

6. Are the figures the same size and shape?

   ○ yes

   ○ no

Line of Symmetry

Circle the correct answer.

1. Tosha draws a house with a line of symmetry. Which house does she draw?

2. Barb finds 2 figures that are the same size and shape. Which 2 figures does she find?

3. Bob finds 2 figures that are the same shape, but not the same size. Which 2 figures does he find?

4. Cameron finds a leaf with a line of symmetry. Which leaf does he find?

Mark the correct answer.

5. Which has a line of symmetry?

6. Which does not have a line of symmetry?

More Symmetry

Write **A, B, C, D, E,** or **F.**

A

B

C

D

E

F

1. Which shape has 3 sides the same length and 3 lines of symmetry?

C

2. Which shape has 3 sides and 1 line of symmetry?

_____

3. Which shape has 4 sides and 1 line of symmetry?

_____

4. Which shape has 4 sides the same length and 4 lines of symmetry?

_____

Mark the correct answer.

5. Which letter has symmetry?

○ V

○ F

○ G

○ Q

6. How many lines of symmetry does the letter **H** have?

○ 0

○ 1

○ 2

○ 3

Moving Figures

Solve.

1. Kira finishes her puzzle. Which shape fits?

2. Dave finishes his puzzle. Should he **turn** or **flip** the shape to make it fit?

_____

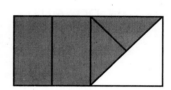

3. Jane has these two shapes. Are they congruent?

_____

4. Does Chris **turn** or **flip** the gray figure to make the white figure?

_____

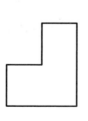

Mark the correct answer.

5. Which word names the move?

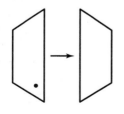

○ turn

○ flip

6. Which word names the move?

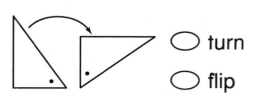

○ turn

○ flip

More About Moving Figures

Solve.

1. Name the move that Ted
used to make this pattern.

flip

2. Name the move that Jill
used to make this pattern.

_____

3. Name the move that Joyce
used to make this pattern.

_____

4. Pete used two different moves
to make this pattern.
What were they?

_____ and _____

Mark the correct answer.

5. Which word names the
move?

$3 \rightarrow 3$

○ turn

○ flip

○ slide

6. Which word names the
move?

$5 \rightarrow 5$

○ turn

○ flip

○ slide

Using Nonstandard Units

Solve.

1. Lin uses 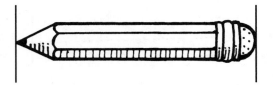 to measure her pencil.
About how many ⬭ long is it?

about ___2___ ⬭

2. Cecil uses ⬭ to measure his train.
About how many ⬭ long is it?

about _____ ⬭

3. Winnie uses ⬭ to measure her leash.
About how many ⬭ long is it?

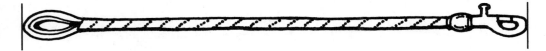

about _____ ⬭

Mark the correct answer.

4. Abby's ribbon is 21 ⬭ long. Susan's ribbon is 12 ⬭ long. Who has the longer ribbon?

◯ Abby

◯ Susan

5. Ben's cat is 25 ⬭ long. Ricky's cat is 27 ⬭ long. Who has the longer cat?

◯ Ben

◯ Ricky

Measuring with Inch Units

Use your inch ruler.
Solve.

1. Rob uses an inch ruler to measure his paintbrush.
About how many inches long is it?

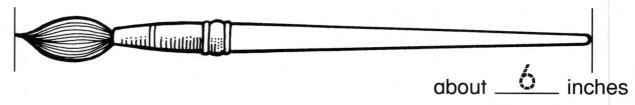

about __**6**__ inches

2. Leslie uses an inch ruler to measure her crayon.
About how many inches long is it?

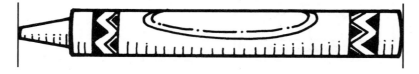

about _____ inches

3. Natasha uses an inch ruler to measure her spoon.
About how many inches long is it?

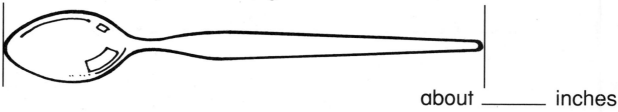

about _____ inches

Mark the correct answer.

4. Carolyn lines up 3 toy cars.
They are 2 inches, 4 inches,
and 5 inches long. How
many inches long are the
three cars together?

   ○ 10   ○ 11

   ○ 12   ○ 13

5. Sherwood lines up 3 pencils.
They are 3 inches, 6 inches,
and 7 inches long. How
many inches long are the
three pencils together?

   ○ 13   ○ 14

   ○ 15   ○ 16

Using an Inch Ruler

Use your inch ruler.
Solve.

1. Ian measures his shoelace.
How many inches long is it?

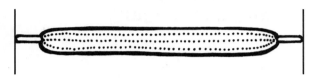

_3_ inches

2. Erika measures a worm.
How many inches long is it?

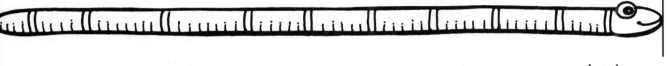

_____ inches

3. Linda measures her pencil.
How many inches long is it?

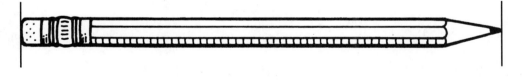

_____ inches

Mark the correct answer.

4. How many inches long is
the chalk?

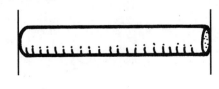

○ 1   ○ 2

○ 3   ○ 4

5. How many inches long is the
paper clip?

○ 1   ○ 2

○ 3   ○ 4

Foot

Use a ruler to measure real things.
Circle **more than I foot** or **less than I foot**.

1. Michele measures the door to her classroom. Is it more than or less than I foot?

   (more than I foot)

   less than I foot

2. Jonathan measures a piece of chalk. Is it more than or less than I foot?

   more than I foot

   less than I foot

3. Mary measures her sandwich. Is it more than or less than I foot?

   more than I foot

   less than I foot

4. Steve measures the teacher's desk. Is it more than or less than I foot?

   more than I foot

   less than I foot

Mark the correct answer.

5. About how long is a banana?

   ◯ less than I foot

   ◯ about I foot

   ◯ more than I foot

6. About how tall is your teacher?

   ◯ less than I foot

   ◯ about I foot

   ◯ more than I foot

Reading Strategy • Make Predictions

Making predictions can help you use guess
and check to solve problems.

A toy robot walks this path.
How long is the path?

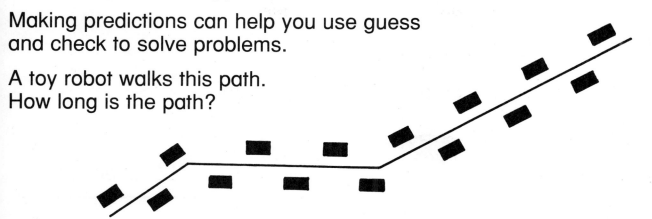

1. Use an inch ruler. Measure 2 parts of the path.

2. Make a prediction. About how long are 3 parts of the path?

_____ inches

3. Check your prediction with a ruler.

The path is ___6___ inches long.

Use making predictions to guess the length.
Then check your guess with a ruler.

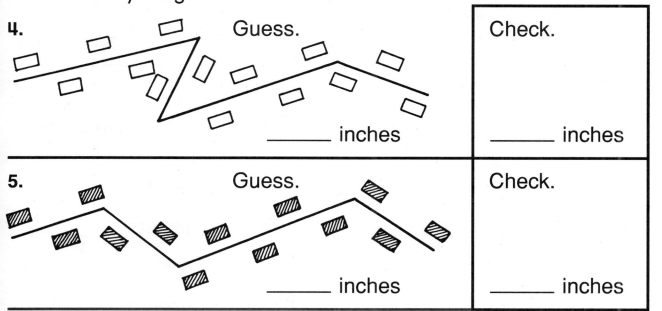

4. Guess.   Check.

_____ inches   _____ inches

5. Guess.   Check.

_____ inches   _____ inches

Centimeters

Use a centimeter ruler.
Write how long.

1. Stan measures a green bean from his garden.

_____6_____ centimeters

---

2. Eric measures a carrot from his garden.

_____ centimeters

---

3. Kenny measures a cucumber from his garden.

_____ centimeters

---

4. Kyle measures a pepper from his garden.

_____ centimeters

Mark the correct answer.

5. How many centimeters long?

◯ 1 centimeter

◯ 2 centimeters

◯ 3 centimeters

6. How many centimeters long?

◯ 2 centimeters

◯ 3 centimeters

◯ 4 centimeters

Decimeters

Use a centimeter ruler. Write how long.
Write **less than, the same as,** or **more than** I decimeter.

I. Judy measures a piece of ribbon.

__9__ centimeters   __less than__ I decimeter

2. Terry measures a piece of string.

_____ centimeters   _____ I decimeter

3. Ben measures a piece of yarn.

_____ centimeters   _____ I decimeter

Mark the correct answer.

4. Which is about
I decimeter long?

○ a new crayon

○ a broom

○ a table

○ a car

5. Which is less than
I decimeter long?

○ a fly

○ a new pencil

○ a desk

○ a cat

Name _____

Exploring Perimeter

1. Use a centimeter ruler.
Measure each side of the square.

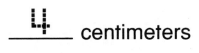 _**4**_ centimeters

_____ centimeters   _____ centimeters

_____ centimeters

---

2. How many centimeters around the square?

_____ + _____ + _____ + _____ = _____ centimeters

How many centimeters around each figure?
Mark the correct answer.

3.

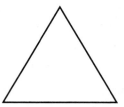

○ 3 centimeters

○ 6 centimeters

○ 9 centimeters

○ 12 centimeters

4.

○ 6 centimeters

○ 12 centimeters

○ 16 centimeters

○ 20 centimeters

Reading Strategy • Make Predictions

Making predictions can help you use guess and
check to solve problems.

Holly uses 1-inch square pieces of cloth to make
a doll quilt. How many squares does she need
to make a quilt the size of the figure?

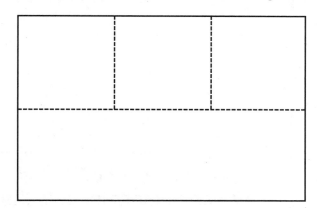

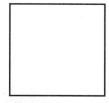

1-inch square

1. How many 1-inch squares will fit in the figure? Look at the
   figure. Make a prediction.

   _____ squares

2. Use 1-inch squares to check your prediction.

3. Solve the problem.

   Holly needs ___6___ 1-inch squares.

Use making predictions to make a guess.
Then use 1-inch squares to check.

4. Rob uses 1-inch square
   pieces of felt to make a rug
   for a model of a log cabin.
   How many squares does
   he need to make a rug the
   size of the figure?

   Guess. _____ squares

   Check. _____ squares

Name _____

Using Cups, Pints, and Quarts

Solve.

1. Abby bought 2 quarts of juice. Sandy bought 3 pints of juice. Who bought more juice?

Abby
_____

2. Jean drank 3 cups of milk. Carl drank 1 pint of milk. Who drank more milk?

_____

3. Is a toothpick **about** 1 centimeter long, **more than** 1 centimeter long, or **less than** 1 centimeter long?

_____
1 centimeter long

4. Lucy has a pencil that is 17 centimeters long. Is the pencil **about** 1 decimeter long, **more than** 1 decimeter long, or **less than** 1 decimeter long?

_____
1 decimeter long

Mark the correct answer.

5. How many pints equal 2 quarts?
   - ○ 1 pint
   - ○ 2 pints
   - ○ 4 pints
   - ○ 8 pints

6. How many cups equal 3 pints?
   - ○ 2 cups
   - ○ 3 cups
   - ○ 6 cups
   - ○ 9 cups

More or Less Than a Pound

Circle the correct answer.

1. Dave buys a new pen. Do you think the pen weighs more or less than 1 pound?

more than 1 pound

(less than 1 pound)

2. Kim eats cereal. Is her spoon more or less than 1 centimeter long?

more than 1 centimeter

less than 1 centimeter

3. Mary measures her shoelaces. Are they more or less than 1 decimeter long?

more than 1 decimeter

less than 1 decimeter

4. Steve plays with his dog. Does the dog weigh more or less than 1 pound?

more than 1 pound

less than 1 pound

Mark the correct answer.

5. Does an ant weigh more than or less than 1 pound?

○ less than 1 pound

○ more than 1 pound

6. Does a bear weigh more than or less than 1 pound?

○ less than 1 pound

○ more than 1 pound

PROBLEM SOLVING   PS113

Using a Thermometer

1. How many degrees warmer was it at 2 o'clock?

8 o'clock   **2 o'clock**

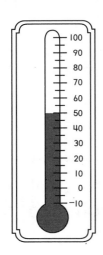 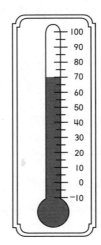

$$\underline{70}\,°F - \underline{50}\,°F = \underline{20}\,°F$$

2. The thermometer shows the temperature outside. The temperature inside is 10° warmer. What is the temperature inside?

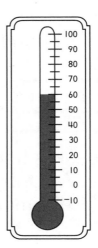

$$\underline{}\,°F + \underline{}\,°F = \underline{}\,°F$$

Mark the correct answer.

3. What is the temperature?

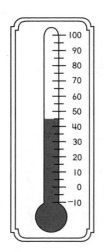

○ 40°F   ○ 41°F

○ 45°F   ○ 55°F

4. What is the temperature?

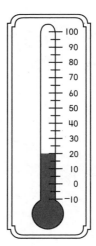

○ 10°F   ○ 20°F

○ 25°F   ○ 30°F

Choosing the Appropriate Tool

Solve.

cup

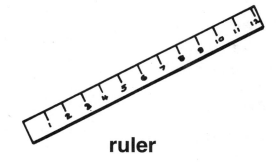

ruler

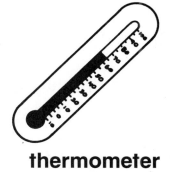

thermometer

1. Edie wants to find out how long a piece of wood is. Which tool does she use?

___ruler___

2. Sam wants to know what the temperature is outside. What tool does he use?

_____

3. Leslie has 4 pints of juice. Tim has 1 quart of juice. Who has more juice?

_____

4. Sam looks at the thermometer outside. What is the temperature?

_____ °F

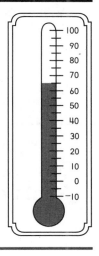

Mark the correct answer.

5. Which tool should Amy use to find out how tall she is?

○ cup

○ ruler

○ thermometer

6. Which tool should Mac use to find out how much milk is in a carton?

○ cup

○ ruler

○ thermometer

Halves and Fourths

Draw a picture.
Circle the correct answer.

1. Tim drank $\frac{1}{2}$ of his cup of milk.

   Nancy drank $\frac{1}{4}$ of her cup of milk.

   Who drank the greater amount?

   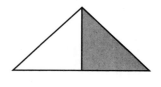   Nancy

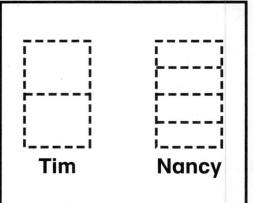

Tim   **Nancy**

2. Ken ate $\frac{1}{4}$ of his brownie.

   Tammy ate $\frac{1}{2}$ of her brownie.

   Who ate less?

   Ken   Tammy

3. Four people share a pizza.
   Each person gets an equal part.
   What part does each person get?

   $\frac{1}{2}$ $\frac{1}{4}$

Mark the correct answer.

4. What part is shaded?

   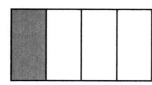

   ○ $\frac{1}{2}$

   ○ $\frac{1}{4}$

5. What part is shaded?

   ○ $\frac{1}{2}$

   ○ $\frac{1}{4}$

Thirds and Sixths

Draw a picture to solve.

1. Tessa drank $\frac{1}{3}$ cup of water and $\frac{1}{6}$ cup of juice. Did she drink more water or juice?

   ___water___

water   juice

2. Zydeco gets $\frac{1}{3}$ can of cat food. Pancake gets $\frac{1}{2}$ can of cat food. Which cat gets less food?

   _____

3. Sporto gets $\frac{1}{4}$ can of dog food. Ginger gets $\frac{1}{2}$ can of dog food. Which dog gets more food?

   _____

Mark the correct answer.

4. What part is shaded?

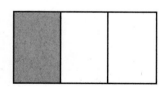

   ○ $\frac{1}{2}$ ○ $\frac{1}{4}$

   ○ $\frac{1}{3}$ ○ $\frac{1}{6}$

5. What part is shaded?

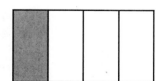

   ○ $\frac{1}{2}$ ○ $\frac{1}{4}$

   ○ $\frac{1}{3}$ ○ $\frac{1}{6}$

More About Fractions

Color to show the fraction.

1. Amy makes a flag that is $\frac{1}{2}$ red and $\frac{1}{2}$ blue.

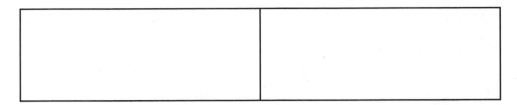

2. Irene makes a flag that is $\frac{1}{4}$ green and $\frac{3}{4}$ yellow.

3. Todd makes a flag that is $\frac{1}{3}$ red and $\frac{2}{3}$ yellow.

Mark the correct answer.

4. Which fraction matches the picture?

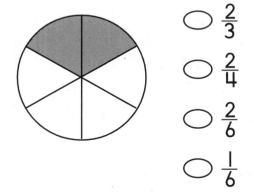

○ $\frac{2}{3}$

○ $\frac{2}{4}$

○ $\frac{2}{6}$

○ $\frac{1}{6}$

5. Which fraction matches the picture?

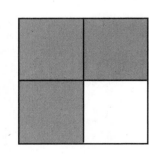

○ $\frac{3}{4}$

○ $\frac{2}{4}$

○ $\frac{1}{4}$

○ $\frac{1}{6}$

Parts of Groups

Draw a picture to solve.

1. Greg picked 4 flowers. 2 flowers are red. What fraction of the flowers are red?

$\left(\dfrac{1}{2}\right)$ $\dfrac{1}{4}$

2. Dirk bought 3 red flowers and 6 yellow flowers. What fraction of the flowers are yellow?

$\dfrac{1}{3}$ $\dfrac{2}{3}$

3. Claire puts $\frac{1}{2}$ cup of water in the red vase. She puts $\frac{1}{4}$ cup of water in the blue vase. Which vase has less water?

red   blue

Mark the correct answer.

4. What fraction is shaded?

○ $\dfrac{1}{2}$

○ $\dfrac{1}{3}$

○ $\dfrac{1}{4}$

○ $\dfrac{1}{6}$

5. What fraction is white?

○ $\dfrac{1}{2}$

○ $\dfrac{1}{3}$

○ $\dfrac{1}{4}$

○ $\dfrac{1}{6}$

Reading Strategy • Use Word Clues

Using word clues can help you solve a problem.

Rick cut an apple pie in fourths. Rick ate 1 piece.

Mike ate 2 pieces. Did they eat $\frac{1}{4}$ or $\frac{3}{4}$ of the pie?

1. Read the problem. Look for word clues.
   How did Rick cut the pie?

   How many pieces did Rick and Mike eat together?

   ___3___ pieces

2. Use fraction circles.
   Make and draw a model.

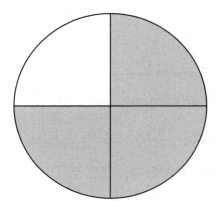

3. Solve the problem. Circle the fraction.

   Rick and Mike ate $\left(\frac{3}{4}\right)$ $\frac{1}{4}$ of the pie.

Use word clues.
Make and draw a model to solve.

4. Sonia cut a cake in sixths.
   Her family ate 3 pieces.

   Did they eat $\frac{1}{6}$ or $\frac{3}{6}$ of the cake?

   $\frac{3}{6}$ $\frac{1}{6}$

Groups of Hundreds

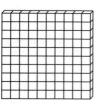 = 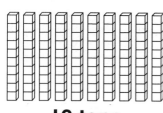 =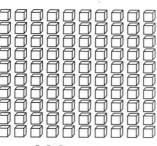

I hundred   =   10 tens   =   100 ones

Solve.

1. There are 100 stamps on a sheet. Vince buys 900 stamps. How many sheets does he buy?

___*9*___ sheets

2. There are 100 pencils in a box. Bud buys 3 boxes. How many pencils does he buy?

_____ pencils

3. There are 100 pieces in a pack of paper. Beth buys 5 packs. How many pieces of paper does she buy?

_____ pieces of paper

4. There are 100 paper clips in a box. Dave buys 700 paper clips. How many boxes does he buy?

_____ boxes

Mark the correct answer.

5. How many tens?

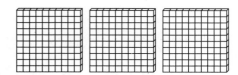

○ 3

○ 30

○ 300

6. How many ones?

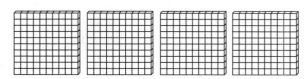

○ 4

○ 40

○ 400

Numbers to 500

Solve. Use the fewest boxes.

1. Mr. Morris buys safety pins for 238 people.
   What does he buy?

   __2__ boxes   __3__ boxes   __8__ single
        of 100   of 10   pins

2. Ms. Webster buys 200 safety pins. What does she buy?

   _____ boxes   _____ boxes   _____ single
        of 100   of 10   pins

3. Yolanda buys 404 safety pins. What does she buy?

   _____ boxes   _____ boxes   _____ single
        of 100   of 10   pins

4. George buys 335 safety pins. What does he buy?

   _____ boxes   _____ boxes   _____ single
        of 100   of 10   pins

Mark the correct answer.

5. Which is the number?

   ○ 246   ○ 462

   ○ 264   ○ 426

6. Which is the number?

   ○ 423   ○ 324

   ○ 432   ○ 342

Numbers to 1,000

Solve. Use the fewest boxes and bags.

1. Martha buys 520 tulip bulbs. What does she buy?

___5___ boxes of 100   ___2___ bags of 10   ___0___ single bulbs

2. Larry buys 903 tulip bulbs. What does he buy?

_____ boxes of 100   _____ bags of 10   _____ single bulbs

3. Sam buys 637 tulip bulbs. What does he buy?

_____ boxes of 100   _____ bags of 10   _____ single bulbs

4. Ray buys 850 tulip bulbs. What does he buy?

_____ boxes of 100   _____ bags of 10   _____ single bulbs

Mark the correct answer.

5. Colleen buys 6 boxes of 100, 4 bags of 10, and 2 single bulbs. How many tulip bulbs does she buy?

○ 246
○ 462
○ 624
○ 642

6. Bradley buys 3 boxes of 100, 8 bags of 10, and 5 single bulbs. How many tulip bulbs does he buy?

○ 358
○ 385
○ 538
○ 583

Name _____

Reading Strategy • Noting Details

Reading for details can help you solve problems.

Mrs. Zydeco has 6 single crayons, 4 boxes of 100 crayons, and 2 boxes of 10 crayons. How many crayons does she have in all?

1. Read the problem carefully to find how many crayons in all.

2. First, find the hundreds. How many boxes of 100 crayons does Mrs. Zydeco have?

_____4_____ boxes of 100 crayons

3. Next, find the tens. How many boxes of 10 crayons does she have?

_____2_____ boxes of 10 crayons

4. Then, find the ones. How many single crayons does she have?

_____6_____ single crayons

5. Solve the problem.

Mrs. Zydeco has _____426_____ crayons.

Solve.

6. Mrs. Smith has 3 boxes of 10 crayons. She has 7 single crayons and 1 box of 100 crayons. How many crayons does Mrs. Smith have?

_____ crayons

7. Ms. Hall has 5 boxes of 100 crayons. She has 4 single crayons. She has no boxes of 10 crayons. How many crayons does Ms. Hall have?

_____ crayons

Building $1.00

Draw and label coins to solve.

1. Bruce has 11 coins that equal
$1.00. Some are dimes. Some
are nickels. How many of each
coin does he have?

___9___ dimes   ___2___ nickels

2. Tina has 1 box of 100 coins, 2 bags
of 10 coins, and 7 single coins. How
many coins does she have in all?

_____ coins

3. David has 4 rolls of 100 pennies and
8 single pennies. How many pennies
does he have?

_____ pennies

4. Neil has 8 coins that equal $1.00.
Some are quarters. Some are
nickels. How many of each coin
does Neil have?

_____ quarters   _____ nickels

Mark the correct answer.

5. How many  equal
$1.00?

◯ 2   ◯ 10

◯ 4   ◯ 25

6. How many  equal
$1.00?

◯ 2   ◯ 10

◯ 4   ◯ 20

Greater Than

Solve.

1. Jessie has 315 pennies.
   James has 355 pennies.
   Who has the greater number
   of pennies?

   _____James_____

2. Opal has 572 nickels. Curtis
   has 525 nickels. Who has
   the greater number of
   nickels?

   _____

3. Molly has 6 coins. Together
   they equal $1.00. What
   coins could she have?

   _____

4. Jim has dimes in his pocket.
   The dimes equal $1.00. How
   many dimes does Jim have?

   _____ dimes

Mark the correct answer.

5. Which is greater?

   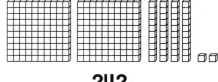

   242

   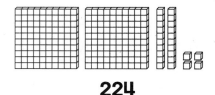

   224

   ◯ 242

   ◯ 224

6. Which is greater?

   ◯ 558

   ◯ 634

7. Which is greater?

   ◯ 346

   ◯ 364

Less Than

Solve.

1. There are 187 cows. There are 157 pigs. Which number of animals is less?

_____157 pigs_____

2. There are 508 bees. There are 580 wasps. Which number of insects is greater?

_____

3. There are 620 elk. There are 602 deer. Which number of animals is less?

_____

4. There are 822 ants. There are 228 termites. Which number of insects is greater?

_____

Mark the correct answer.

5. Which is less?

107

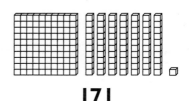

171

○ 107

○ 171

6. Which is less?

○ 832

○ 881

7. Which is less?

○ 675

○ 567

Greater Than and Less Than

Write > or < in the circle.
Solve.

1. There are 562 adults and 652 children at the zoo. Are there more adults or children at the zoo?

$$562 \;\textcircled{<}\; 652$$

children

2. The zoo sold 218 bags of peanuts and 281 bags of popcorn. Were more bags of peanuts or popcorn sold?

$$218 \;\bigcirc\; 281$$

_____

3. On Tuesday 716 children visited the park. On Wednesday 709 children visited. Which day did fewer children visit the park?

$$716 \;\bigcirc\; 709$$

_____

4. There are 462 birds at the town park. There are 284 birds at the city park. Are there fewer birds at the town park or the city park?

$$462 \;\bigcirc\; 284$$

_____

Mark the correct answer.

5. Choose **greater** or **less**.

505 is _____ than 550.

○ greater

○ less

6. Choose > or <.

$$200 \;\bigcirc\; 20$$

○ >

○ <

Before, After, and Between

 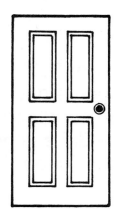  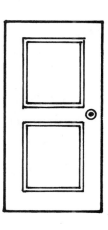

779   781   782

Solve.

1. Pete's room is just after 782. What number is his room?

_783_

2. Sara's room is 779. Theo's room is 782. Which number is greater?

_____

3. Jason's room number is between 779 and 781. What is his room number?

_____

4. Kyle has 62 marbles. Stan has 70 marbles. Who has fewer marbles?

_____

Mark the correct answer.

5. Which number is just before 220?

○ 210

○ 212

○ 219

○ 221

6. Which number comes between?

489, _____, 491

○ 409

○ 490

○ 498

○ 500

Ordering Sets of Numbers

Solve.

1. Wendy scored 178 points, 182 points, and 172 points bowling. Write the number of points in order from least to greatest.

<u>172</u>, <u>178</u>, <u>182</u>

2. Kate got 202 points in her first game and 220 points in her second game. In which game did she get the greater number of points?

_____

3. Joseph scored 172, 105, 155, and 150 points. Write the number of points in order from least to greatest.

_____, _____, _____, _____

4. Maggie scored 187 points in her first game and 178 points in her second game. In which game did she score fewer points?

_____

Mark the correct answer.

5. Which numbers are in order from least to greatest?

○ 642, 604, 644, 620

○ 620, 604, 642, 644

○ 604, 642, 620, 644

○ 604, 620, 642, 644

6. Which numbers are in order from least to greatest?

○ 809, 890, 908, 980

○ 809, 890, 980, 908

○ 890, 908, 809, 980

○ 908, 980, 809, 890

Modeling Addition of Three-Digit Numbers

Use Workmat 5 and 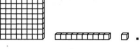 .
Add.

---

1. Bob ordered 144 bottles of orange juice and 248 bottles of grape juice for his store. How many bottles did he order?

392 bottles

2. Cameron ordered 636 stuffed dogs and 227 stuffed cats for his toy store. How many stuffed animals did he order?

_____ stuffed animals

---

3. Barb ordered 415 red beads and 239 white beads to make jewelry. Did she order fewer red or white beads?

_____ beads

4. Craig ordered 278 roses and 319 daisies for his flower shop. Did he order more roses or daisies?

_____

Mark the correct answer.

5. Mr. Curtis drove 649 miles one week and 234 miles the next week. How many miles did he drive in all?

- ◯ 873
- ◯ 875
- ◯ 883
- ◯ 973

6. Mrs. Fox drove 168 miles one week and 518 miles the next week. How many miles did she drive in all?

- ◯ 676
- ◯ 678
- ◯ 686
- ◯ 688

Adding Three-Digit Numbers

Add.

1. Mrs. Dehmel read 252 pages in her book on Monday. She read 175 pages on Tuesday. How many pages did she read in the two days?

   __427__ pages

2. There are 137 children in Grade 2. There are 125 children in Grade 1. How many children are there in both grades together?

   _____ children

3. Mac watches two movies. The first is 134 minutes long. The second is 185 minutes long. How long are both movies together?

   _____ minutes

4. Dorothy has 426 pennies in one jar. She has 116 pennies in another jar. How many pennies does she have in all?

   _____ pennies

Mark the correct answer.

5. Alex has 2 pouches of marbles. There are 144 marbles in each pouch. How many marbles does he have in all?

   ○ 144

   ○ 244

   ○ 288

   ○ 388

6. Kristin has 2 sticker books. There are 155 stickers in one book. There are 125 stickers in the other book. How many stickers does she have in all?

   ○ 318

   ○ 308

   ○ 218

   ○ 280

Modeling Subtraction of Three-Digit Numbers

Use Workmat 5 and 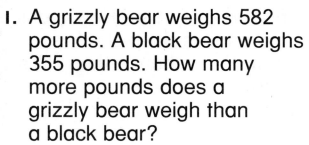 .
Solve.

I. A grizzly bear weighs 582 pounds. A black bear weighs 355 pounds. How many more pounds does a grizzly bear weigh than a black bear?

<u>227</u> more pounds

2. The baby bear weighs 157 pounds. The mother bear weighs 314 pounds more than the baby. How many pounds does the mother bear weigh?

_____ pounds

3. A black bear weighs 382 pounds. A polar bear weighs 572 pounds more. How many pounds does a polar bear weigh?

_____ pounds

4. The mother polar bear weighs 878 pounds. The baby polar bear weighs 365 pounds. How many more pounds does the mother weigh than the baby?

_____ more pounds

Mark the correct answer.

5. The second grade collected 542 cans of food. The first grade collected 214 cans. How many more cans did the second grade collect than the first grade?

◯ 328

◯ 332

◯ 328

◯ 756

6. There are 984 children at East School. There are 738 children at West School. How many more children are there at East School than West School?

◯ 256

◯ 254

◯ 246

◯ 244

Subtracting Three-Digit Numbers

Solve.

1. Mr. Smith drove 865 miles in May. He drove 748 miles in June. How many more miles did he drive in May than in June?

_117_ more miles

2. Judy lives 458 miles from Rick's house and 309 miles from Bill's house. How many more miles does she live from Rick's house than Bill's house?

_____ more miles

3. Ms. Marvin drives 115 miles on Monday and 204 miles on Tuesday. How many miles does she drive in all?

_____ miles

4. Chuck drives 326 miles one week. He drives 135 miles the next week. How many miles does he drive in both weeks together?

_____ miles

Mark the correct answer.

5. There were 952 children at the zoo. Then 526 children went home. How many children were left at the zoo?

○ 436

○ 434

○ 426

○ 424

6. There are 827 adults at the fair. There are 441 children. How many more adults than children are there?

○ 486

○ 426

○ 386

○ 326

Name _____

Reading Strategy • Use Word Clues

Using word clues can help you solve problems.

Michele buys a puzzle for $2.47 and a ball for $1.82. How much does she spend to buy both toys?

Jonathan spends $8.90 on a plane and $2.75 on a kite. How much more does the plane cost than the kite?

1. Read the problem. Look for word clues that tell you to add or to subtract.

The word **both** tells you to add both prices.

The words **how much more** tell you to compare prices and subtract.

2. Add or subtract.

$$\begin{array}{r} \$2.47 \\ + 1.82 \\ \hline \$4.29 \end{array}$$

$$\begin{array}{r} \$8.90 \\ - 2.75 \\ \hline \$6.15 \end{array}$$

3. Solve the problem.

Michele spends __$4.29__ to buy both toys.

The plane costs __$6.15__ more than the kite.

Look for word clues. Add or subtract.

4. Robin buys a toy rabbit for $6.82 and a toy cat for $9.46. How much more does the cat cost than the rabbit?

_____

5. Jason spends $3.72 for a kite and $5.65 for a drum. How much does he spend to buy both?

_____

Adding Equal Groups

Draw a picture.
Write how many in all.

1. Each car has 4 wheels. How many wheels on 2 cars? ___4___ + ___4___ = ___8___ wheels	
2. Each bicycle has 2 wheels. How many wheels on 3 bicycles? ___ + ___ + ___ = ___ wheels	
3. Each tricycle has 3 wheels. How many wheels on 3 tricycles? ___ + ___ + ___ = ___ wheels	
4. Each truck has 8 wheels. How many wheels on 2 trucks? ___ + ___ = ___ wheels	

Mark the correct answer.

5. Each truck has 8 wheels.
   How many wheels on 3
   trucks?

   $8 + 8 + 8 =$ _____

   ○ 8
   ○ 16
   ○ 24
   ○ 32

6. There are 6 eggs in each
   carton. How many eggs in
   3 cartons?

   $6 + 6 + 6 =$ _____

   ○ 3
   ○ 6
   ○ 12
   ○ 18

Multiplying with 2 and 5

Write the sum.
Then write the product.

1. There are 2 nests. There
are 4 eggs in each nest.
How many eggs are there?

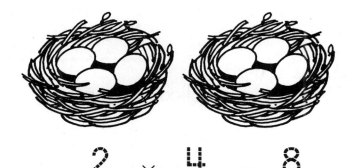

$$\underline{\quad 4 \quad} + \underline{\quad 4 \quad} = \underline{\quad 8 \quad} \qquad \underline{\quad 2 \quad} \times \underline{\quad 4 \quad} = \underline{\quad 8 \quad}$$

---

2. There are 3 trees. There are
4 birds in each tree. How
many birds are there?

$$\underline{\quad} + \underline{\quad} + \underline{\quad} = \underline{\quad} \qquad \underline{\quad\quad} \times \underline{\quad\quad} = \underline{\quad\quad}$$

---

3. There are 5 apples. There are
2 worms in each apple. How
many worms are there?

$$\underline{\quad} + \underline{\quad} + \underline{\quad} + \underline{\quad} + \underline{\quad} = \underline{\quad} \qquad \underline{\quad\quad} \times \underline{\quad\quad} = \underline{\quad\quad}$$

Mark the correct answer.

4. Which number sentence
matches the picture?

- ○ $2 + 5 = 7$
- ○ $2 \times 5 = 10$
- ○ $5 \times 5 = 25$

5. Which number sentence
matches the picture?

- ○ $3 \times 3 = 9$
- ○ $5 \times 3 = 15$
- ○ $5 \times 5 = 25$

Multiplying with 3 and 4

Adults $5
Children $4

Soda $2
Popcorn $3

Draw a model.
Write the multiplication sentence.

1. Kay buys tickets for 2 adults.
   How much does she spend?

   __2__ × __5__ = $__10__

2. Norma buys tickets for 4 children.
   How much does she spend?

   _____ × _____ = $_____

3. Jon buys sodas for Jack, Stan, and
   himself. How much does he pay?

   _____ × _____ = $_____

4. Mr. Lee buys 5 boxes of popcorn.
   How much does he spend?

   _____ × _____ = $_____

Mark the correct answer.

5. Marisol buys 3 boxes of
   popcorn. How much does
   she spend?

   ◯ $9
   ◯ $16
   ◯ $20
   ◯ $25

6. José buys tickets for 3
   children. How much does
   he spend?

   ◯ $10
   ◯ $12
   ◯ $14
   ◯ $16

Reading Strategy • Recognize Patterned Text

Looking for word patterns can help you solve problems.

| There are 2 cats. Each cat has 4 legs. How many legs in all do the 2 cats have? | There are 3 dogs. Each dog has 2 ears. How many ears in all do the 3 dogs have? |

1. Look for word patterns in the problems.
Each problem tells how many groups.

__2__ cats   __3__ dogs

Each problem tells how many in each group.

__4__ legs   __2__ ears

2. Draw a picture.

3. Write a multiplication sentence. Solve.

__2__ × __4__ = __8__ legs   __3__ × __2__ = __6__ ears

Look for word patterns. Draw a picture.
Then multiply to solve.

4. There are 4 raccoons. Each raccoon has 4 paws. How many paws in all do the 4 raccoons have?

_____ × _____ = _____ paws

5. There are 5 horses. Each horse has 2 eyes. How many eyes in all do the 5 horses have?

_____ × _____ = _____ eyes

How Many in Each Group?

Use Workmat 1 and ▢.
Make equal groups.
Write how many are in each group.

1. There are 9 people. There are 3 cars. The same number of people ride in each car. How many are in each car?

____3____ people

2. Carol has 10 model cars. She gives an equal number of cars to each of 5 friends. How many cars does she give to each friend?

_____ cars

3. Bill has 15 model cars. He has 5 shelves. He puts the same number of cars on each shelf. How many are on each shelf?

_____ cars

4. There are 16 people. There are 4 cars. There is an equal number of people in each car. How many people are in each car?

_____ people

Mark the correct answer.

5. There are 12 people in 4 cars. There is an equal number of people in each car. How many people are in each car?

○ 3
○ 4
○ 12
○ 16

6. Leigh has 8 books. She has 4 shelves. She puts on equal number of books on each shelf. How many books are on each shelf?

○ 2
○ 4
○ 8
○ 12

How Many Equal Groups?

Use Workmat 1 and ⬜.
Put an equal number in each group.
Write how many groups.

1. There are 15 children in the swim club. There are 5 children on each team. How many teams are there?

_____3_____ teams

2. There are 20 children in music class. The teacher puts 5 children in each group. How many groups are there?

_____ groups

3. There are 8 baseball teams. 2 teams play on each baseball field. How many baseball fields are there?

_____ baseball fields

4. There are 18 baseball players. There are 9 players on each team. How many teams are there?

_____ teams

Mark the correct answer.

5. Susan has 6 baseballs. She puts 3 baseballs in each bag. How many bags does she use?

○ 2
○ 3
○ 6
○ 12

6. David has 12 baseball cards. He puts 4 cards on each page of his album. How many pages does he use?

○ 3
○ 4
○ 12
○ 16

Reading Strategy • Recognize Patterned Text

Darrell has 15 dog biscuits and 3 dogs.
He gives an equal number of biscuits
to each dog. How many biscuits does
each dog get?

1. The problem tells how many biscuits in all.

   __15__ dog biscuits

2. The problem tells how many dogs.

   __3__ dogs

3. The problem asks how many
   biscuits does each dog get?
   Draw a picture to solve.

   Each dog gets _____ biscuits.

Look for word patterns.
Draw a picture to solve.

4. Merry has 9 carrots. She has 3 rabbits.
   She gives each rabbit the same
   number of carrots. How many carrots
   does each rabbit get?

   _____ carrots

5. Jim cuts an apple into 8 pieces. He
   gives an equal number of pieces to
   each of his 4 pet guinea pigs. How
   many pieces does each guinea
   pig get?

   _____ pieces

Reading Strategy • Visualize

Picturing a problem in your mind can help you solve the problem.

Helen has a bag of 20 peanuts. She gives an equal number of peanuts to each of 5 elephants. How many peanuts does each elephant get?

1. Read the problem.
Try to picture the peanuts and the elephants.

2. Think about how the peanuts could be divided into 5 equal groups.

3. Draw circles around equal groups of peanuts to show how many peanuts each elephant will get.

4. Solve.

Each elephant gets ____4____ peanuts.

Think about the problem.
Draw a picture or make a model to solve.

5. There are 18 bananas and 6 monkeys. Each monkey gets an equal number of bananas. How many bananas does each monkey get?

_____ bananas

6. There are 16 balloons and 8 children. Each child gets an equal number of balloons. How many balloons does each child get?

_____ balloons